Cultivating a
Culture of Caring

by Mark A Hardin

TABLE OF CONTENT

Foreword by Jim Hohnberger
Forward by Dwight L Hardin
Acknowledgements
Preface
Introduction`

Content

Forward by *Jim Hohnberger*

As I lay in my hospital bed, with two broken vertebrae, five fractured ribs, and a collapsed lung, in walks Marc with flowers in his hand.

"Marc, what ever are you doing here?"

I couldn't believe it. I hardly knew Marc. How did he find out I was in the hospital? Why would he take the time to see me and go to the expense of bringing me a gift?

Then Marc awkwardly approached my bed, probably because of the five other people in the room. He stood by my side and in a choked voice, as well as tears in his eyes, said, "You have done so much for me – you will never understand what meeting you has done for me." Then with shyness, awkwardly departed.

Sally and I hardly knew Marc, but God had asked us to wrap our arms around him and his girlfriend. They were purchasing our ministry home office, located on 13 acres in the country. They just loved the location, setting, and the home. We had thought God would bring us a couple "worthy" of what this property represented. Marc and his girlfriend having no religious affiliation were living together without the benefit of matrimony. Yet, God impressed us to just, "Love them without an 'If'". No prejudice, no lectures, just show you really care for them…period.

This was their first home, so we accommodated them in every way possible. Showing lots of interest in them personally. We left some extras, not originally included in the sale, to get them started. An office desk and chair, dinette set, La-Z-Boy rocker, lawn mower, hoses and sprinkler, garden tools, and two books. "Escape To God" and "Irresistible". The latter being a book on marriage.

God evidently used this care package, this "Love without an 'If'", to not only touch their lives but to give them new direction.

We firmly believe God seldom brings two people together for the benefit of just one. Now Marc is standing next to me, tears in his eyes and a choked up voice saying, "I care about you".

That's what this book, "Cultivating a Culture of Caring" is all about! One life touching another life, saying, "I'm here for YOU", period!

That's what God did for you and me, and it is what He calls us to as well. "By this shall all men know." John 13:35

As you read "Cultivating a Culture of Caring" the Holy Spirit will be whispering His suggestions to your conscience. Please write down His invitation to do unto others as you would have them do unto you, and God will be glorified!

Jim Hohnberger
Empowered Living Ministries
Author/Speaker

Foreword by Dad…Dwight L Hardin

Mark Anthony Hardin was born in September 1961 to Dwight and Martha Hardin. He was a miracle baby!

Dr. Wilson said he could find no heartbeat before the birth. Two weeks before the birth, he said that the baby would be stillborn and that we (Dwight and Martha Hardin) would just wait for the natural birth. On September 17th, we were having communion in our church. My dad, our pastor, told Martha that when you take this communion, you'll feel movement in your womb.

True to the prophecy, the instant she received the wine and the bread, the baby kicked. She ran back to the seat where I was standing and put my hand upon her belly and I felt it. He was kicking so we both were crying. We immediately headed for the hospital 20 miles away. Unexpectedly Martha was in labor for 18 hours. Dr. Wilson said to Martha, "Martha, it's too late to take the baby Caesarean. You are too weak, but there are a lot of people out there praying for you. You and I, we're going to hold hands and pray. And you give it all you've got." Instantly the baby began to emerge, but he was breech and the naval cord was wrapped around his neck three times. But the doctor was able to stretch the cord enough to cut it and get him out of the womb. So on September 18, 1961, Mark was born a natural birth. We knew that God had spared him for special reasons. He received the Holy Ghost at age 12, and was baptized at the age of 10. As most of us have, Mark has had his good times and his bad times. He has faced much adversity at times, but has grown in the Lord through it all. It is his life's experiences that have prompted him to write this book, Cultivating a Culture of Caring. My hope is that you will, by reading this book, be blessed, encouraged, and inspired to help others around you. We need to be aware of the spiritual, physical, and financial struggles of others and be willing to help. If all of us were encouragers, it would be a wonderful world to live in.

Dwight L. Hardin
Pastor/Evangelist/Soulwinner/my dad

ACKNOWLEDGEMENTS

To say that I give thanks to God would be an understatement! In fact, words cannot express my gratitude to my Lord and Savior for what He has done. This book is only a glimpse into His grace and mercy shown in my life.

As I reflect back over the years and how this book developed in my heart and then became a burden, many should be recognized. But, time and space will limit me to only the following.

To Jesus Christ, my Lord, I give you thanks for allowing me to be an instrument in your kingdom.

To my lovely and dear wife, Ronda, thank you for enduring me!

To my parents for their continual encouragement.

Thank you to Jim Hohnberger, of Empowered Living Ministries, for reviewing this book and providing a forward. Jim and his wife Sally are renown authors and speakers. His first book, "Escape To God" is a must read.

To the following men that God has allowed to be a strength and encouragement throughout the trials that led up to the writing of this book and beyond. Thank you Bishop William Sciscoe, Bishop Jeff Smith, Pastor Jack Stoops, Pastor Tim Estes, and Pastor Tracy Zimmerman. During the lowest time of my life you cared enough to reach out to me.

To my children, Miranda and Kevin Tipsword (and grandbaby Karson Joel), and Micah Hardin, I love you very much! I give thanks every day that God brought you into my life. Thank you for being there even in the times that you did not understand what I was going through. God is faithful, and He has shown to be our Rock and Fortress.

In Christ Alone,
Mark A Hardin

PREFACE

It was the darkest time of my life, to this point, when I received a call from an "old" Bible College acquaintance. After asking how I was doing, to which I put on the usual facade and said "Terrific!", he then said that he felt the Lord had impressed him to call me to come and minister at the church in Clute TX. The emotions flooded in, the facade fell off, my heart ached with a piercing pain once again as I began to sob and weakly responded, "Jeff, you don't want me. I have nothing to offer." Bishop Jeff Smith's tone changed on the phone as he then began to understand why God had placed me on his heart.

Longer story short. for the first time in my life, my wife and I were flown to Texas, treated like royalty, and as the time drew nearer for me to minister to around forty ministry leaders, department heads, and their spouses, I felt the weight of humility pressing upon me. I was overwhelmed that anyone would want me even around, let alone have me speak. How could I encourage or direct a group of people while I myself felt that I was a disastrous failure. Besides, several very close mentors have already told me I was not called to do this type of ministry.

As I prayed and thoughts bounced around in my mind like a pinball machine, pinging from one side to another…thoughts scattered with no focus as I wrestled with this calling! I started with one theme only to end up on another for several weeks.

Then, as I stepped to the podium all of the thoughts from the past several days and weeks seemed to fade away, leaving me with only one old chorus that goes like this;

> *Just let me walk with you Jesus.*
> *Don't ever leave me alone.*
> *For without you I could never,*
> *no never make heaven my home.*

Simple as it seems, it was the prayer of my heart crying out, and God used it to spring into a three and one half hour time of prayer, supplication, deliverance, and prophetic words through those in attendance.

On the Monday following a powerful weekend, that could only be ordained by the Lord Himself, the inspiration began to fall to create a series of thoughts to share called "Cultivating a Culture of Caring"

Shortly after, another individual spoke a prophetic word to me that was so very on target. After making five points that could not be denied that God knew exactly where I was at, he then said, "…and write that book!" Not knowing me, he could not know that I had been feeling that eventually the series/seminar would evolve into a book.

God knows where you are at! He knows exactly where you are…at this moment…no matter the condition. No matter who has told you, in word or deed, that you are a failure and have implied that God doesn't need you. Let me assure you, God knows your condition and He still loves and cares about you!

One other song has guided me these many years, and it goes like this;

> To be used of God, to speak to sing, to pray.
> To be used of God, to show someone the way.
> Oh, how I long so much, just to feel the touch,
>   of His consuming power.
> To be used of God, is my desire.

God is concerned about every soul, and, His desire is for us to care for them all. "Red, yellow, black, or white. They are precious in His sight…" Rich or poor. Old or young. No matter what they look like, smell like, act like, or what they have done in their past or present, God wants us to reach out to them and show them that "He Cares". It will be through our touch that God becomes connected to a lost and dying world.

Caring does not come natural.

It behooves us to cultivate, or create the environment, for a caring attitude to grow.

INTRODUCTION

Jim climbed to the top of a stack of inner tubes, steadied by several trustworthy helpers, and he began to bark out the instruction. "Stay together! If someone looses their floatation device in the rapids, go to them and help them while someone else retrieves their inner tube. We are in this together!! Everybody ready to go?!"

My son and I had made a 36hr trip to the North Fork of the Flathead River, just west of the Glacier Mountains, to meet with some new found friends. One of the activities was to float our inner tubes down three rapids that had some substantial drops that would dip you down far enough to submerge and dislodge you from your inner tube. The instruction was sound advice just in case someone would fall off and need help, which several did.

I recall one young girl falling in and within a second several of us paddled vigorously in the current to her aid, while others went to capture her inner tube. Once through the rapids, she was safely back on and ready for the remainder of the ride.

As my mind drifts back, drawing from the fond memories of the trip my son and I took to Montana, the floats down the mountain stream was one of the highlights. The lesson learned from the adventurous rides down the rapids reminded me of how interlocked humanity really is. Having met all of these folks in just the last day or two, still there was a sense of responsibility to "my brother". If they fell in, I determined to help…as did they, if I were to need a helping hand.

Cain ask the question, "Am I my brother's keeper?" To which all of eternity screams a resounding response of "YES!!" For really, that is a fundamental principle that God has set in place, even in our fallen state of humanity, that we are to care for our brother.

This book has been a work in progress since the beginning of time…it didn't just start with my feeble attempt to explain the burden that has been placed on my heart. Since the time of Eve sharing the fruit from the tree of The Knowledge of Good and Evil, God has cared about humanity and their well being. He placed that same inspiration in every human born into this world since. It is up to us to determine if we will cultivate the caring spirit toward our fellow man.

When someone falls into the turbulent waters of life, being tossed about by currents that desire to drag them below the surface, it is our responsibility to reach to them and lend a hand.

It will require a lot of energy! I recall how sore I was after just a couple of floats down a mile or so stretch of rapids. It was difficult enough saving my self…keeping my feet down stream from my head so I could watch and navigate over the large boulders and ensuing drop offs, then the splash as I was submerged only to pop back up as I held tightly to my tube. Then, to look over and see another that has fallen off…immediately the instincts of "I need to help" went into action as I would dig deep into the current and work my way toward someone I didn't even know.

Cultivating a Culture of Caring will require work. Just as with a garden where weeds are pulled and blisters swell up from the use of a hoe, we find this caring business causing a lot of selfless work. A farmer will not last long if they do not cultivate a culture that enhances growth in a field. So it is with a culture, that seems to be so contrary to our society, where we must push our selves to create an environment that cares for others. Love thy neighbor as thy self…who would have ever thought of such a concept…

I pray that you are challenged and inspired to cultivate a culture of caring in your personal life, and in doing so, inspiring others to care as well.

Clarified Purpose

Some will misinterpret my intent as a license to fail without consequences, while others will perceive that we cannot condemn sin. Both would be incorrect interpretations of the need to cultivate a culture of caring.

   Just because we need to encourage forgiveness and reaching to those who have fallen into temptations, it is not a passive Gospel that condones the actions.

As you have heard on many occasions, we should "hate the sin but love the sinner". It is certainly applicable here. Our principles remain rooted in the Word of God, yet, no matter what the circumstances, or the sin, we reach to the one who has fallen.

Wisdom should always be used to protect from becoming involved in a situation that may compromise your beliefs or causes one to veer away from Biblical principles. Especially when dealing with someone of the opposite sex or snares that can entrap or make you vulnerable to slander. Again, wisdom is needed that we must receive from God to protect the innocent. It is a part of the cultivating process as well to know when and how to reach. But, it cannot stop us from reaching!

HOW IS YOUR VIEW OF HUMANITY?

CHAPTER 1

It is imperative that I bring the theme into focus very quickly. Throughout the thoughts, though at times scattered about, I will attempt to express what God has laid on my heart, I do not want us to miss the one challenge that we must walk away with. If there is any provocation that could be gained, I pray that we understand how much God loves every single soul. For no other reason than that He loves, therefore it is settled by His own will that we too should love and care for every soul. For, in reality His view of a soul is much greater than what we could ever imagine.

God's View Of A Soul

> *Lamentations 4:1-2*, *"How is the gold become dim! the most pure gold changed! the stones of the sanctuary poured out at the top of all the streets! The sons of Zion, so precious, comparable to fine gold, how are they esteemed as earthen pitchers, the work of the hands of the potter!"*

We must be careful with how we view those around us!

One commentary declared that the prophet literally meant that men were worth their weight equal to gold, but had been reduced to their weight equal to a broken piece of pottery. The contrast in value is not comprehensive! How could we calculate the difference in value? No comparisons could be ran! Each soul is more precious than all the gold in this world. Yet, we relegate each soul as nothing more valuable than a broken piece of glass.

God's Economy

The value of any material good is based on one commodity. Gold! The price of my home has to do with what the market can sustain in our area, but, the number of dollars it takes to purchase it is based on what that dollar represents in gold. The stronger the dollar, the fewer it takes to purchase an ounce of gold. The weaker the dollar, it will take more of them to purchase an ounce of gold. The whole economy is based on what the Dollar, Yen,

Euro, etc will purchase in the gold market.

It is ironic to me that Heaven's streets will be paved with gold…just something to think about for a moment. The very thing that brings value on this earth…the basis of our economy will be pavement in Heaven!

Take note that the passage in Lamentations, that we've read, draws a comparison between fine gold (so refined that it is as clear as glass), we see that God would compare it to a soul. One soul! May I propose that Heaven's economy is based on the most valued commodity, that being, a single soul. The whole economy of Heaven is based on the value of a soul. What a revelatory understanding! If we can only see every person through God's economic system we will truly understand why He would go to such lengths to reach to every soul.

Use Leads To Abuse

In this sinful state, in which we dwell each day, the greatest atrocity is that we tend to view human life as nothing more than something to use, only to discard when it is no longer useful. Or so we think! On a whim even a child can be destroyed in the last stages prior to birth. Because it will "cramp the parent's style" the child is viewed as a "cancer" that needs to be removed before it becomes worse.

Marriages are dissolved. Children are abused. Gangs flourish. Women are raped. Children molested. Pornography exploits the modesty, purity, and dignity of all that they touch. It is acceptable to jump from one partner to another…or multiples if one desires. Why not, they have no worth other than my pleasure…right?

Business cut backs. Kick out the life time employee just months before their retirement obligations would be complete. It's just another number that jeopardized the bottom line. Neighbors are annoyances. Time is too valuable to use for a friend. Racial and social divides erupt on every corner, creeping into the congregations everywhere. Disdain for the weakest among us becomes the norm. Love your neighbor is always followed by the question of "Who is my neighbor?". Who has the time to build a relationship? Text me your problems, so I can decide if I wish to respond, or make an excuse that it never came through.

Saints are stupid. Pastors are old and no longer "in touch". Boards and Elders rise up to control. Pastors do not need their hands tied by members that disagree. Jealousy causes leaders to cast out one that is no longer needed or doesn't agree on every point. Power struggles that have cast servant hood into the dung pile.

Let brotherly love continue? Why, that's too time consuming!

Who needs to communicate? It's a bore listening to their opinions or concepts when mine are so awesome!

Perspectives are not my priority, unless their mine. Don't you know that I am in direct contact with the Most High…see how I glow when I enter the room! Keep your open dialog and quality time. If you were really spiritual you would be on the same level as me…read my mind and do as I think.

√ All because of a flawed view of humanity!

All the while, failing to look through the lens, that God uses , when looking at fallen mankind. We can use the piece of pottery as long as it will hold water, or serve my purpose. But, when it is found to have a flaw then it is thrown out the back door with the rest of the useless junk that we've discarded. God forbid! Oh, that we could see that a soul is as a golden heirloom worth more than all the worldly gain.

My deepest prayer is that God will help me more than anyone else to gain His heartbeat, so that I can view every soul through His eyes.

A Bean In A Boot

Have you ever had a bean in your boot? I have. While cleaning out grain bins you have to climb up the outside of the bin, squeeze through a trap door in the roof, climb back down into the depths of the bin, begin to scoop grain until you can open the doorway closer to the ground. Its dusty, dim, and eerie…I always dread the first 30-40 minutes of being inside a bin while it is all closed in with only the small access in the roof. I am always grateful when the side door is open enough that you can crawl out without going back up the side to exit!

By the time you get the pile of beans down to the floor, where the auger sweep can be set up, and start the final removal of grain, your boot always has at least one bean that has worked its way down to the inner sole, to become simply an irritation. That bean, like a small pebble in your shoe, will keep crying out "I'm here!" every time you take another step!! It will remain an irritation until you address it!

This has been my experience with this thought of "Cultivating a Culture of Caring"! It wouldn't go away until it was dealt with. Our friends, family, loved ones, co-workers, neighbors, church family, and even our enemies need us to cultivate a habit of caring. It is imperative as "Christians", especially, to cultivate a culture that will show forth the love of Christ in that He first cared for us…when we were unlovable.

Strive For Solutions

My pastor, Rev. R Kidder, told me on several occasions, "Leaders never bring a problem without bringing at least one solution to recommend". This thought has stuck with me over the years, and I've tried to live by the proverb, even though some did not appreciate it as much as I.

It behooves us to seek out problems, for the root cause is always below the surface and is not readily identified. But, once we have dug down and found where the origin is, we then have to be prepared to present solutions for eliminating the thing that is causing the "fruit" to spoil.

Many times we look at the "fruit" and try to diagnose a resulting imperfection, instead of the actual problem…this may provide some patchwork for a period of time, and you may feel that the right solution has been diagnosed, but, eventually it will erupt again and usually with even more vigor than before.

It will be my earnest desire to not only point out problematic areas, but, to also seek to find the root cause. The journey to finding a solution, that will heal the issue, is sometimes painful when we have to look at ourselves to see how we have de-valued humanity through our actions. But, the self-inspection will be worth the journey!

Our solutions cannot be found without first getting serious about getting to the root cause. As the same wise pastor told me, "The answers lie in the questions you don't want to ask!". I have found this to be so true. We tend to avoid the areas that need an interrogator's light shown on it. The areas that are the root cause are usually the very flaws we've tried to hide for years…you've heard it said, "The definition of insanity is doing the same things over and over, expecting different results" Ego must be set aside…"sacred cows" must be sacrificed…otherwise, we will never address the negative affect.

So, let's strive for solutions, by being honest with ourselves first. Our response cannot be, "That's the way we've always done it". We will never attempt to cultivate if we like the way we've always done it, but still hate the results. We will attempt to spotlight with the light of the Holy Script to illuminate areas that have been ignored. Truly there is nothing new under the sun…the same issues we have today have been exampled in Scripture for several thousand years. We just need to open our hearts and mind as we dive into the depths of the Word, so that we will change into its likeness.

Practice Makes What?

The old adage, "Practice Makes Perfect" is not correct. If you practice the wrong things, you will always entrench the wrong habits, continuing to get the wrong results. The proverb is better stated, "Perfect Practice Makes Perfect"…find what is right, then practice doing it until we've got the right results.

If we have a revolving door and find that we are gaining new people but always seem to be loosing the same amount each year…growth is stymied because we can't stop the bleeding, then perhaps it could be that we need to Cultivate our ability to Care for those who have been placed in our care.

Let us continue our journey into "Cultivating a Culture of Caring" by looking at the process of preparing the ground…

CHAPTER 2

We all know people who know that everyone else is the problem. I could use many examples, but, in every group there is that person, or persons, who think everyone else has a problem and have never found that the splinter in someone else's eye is not nearly as prominent as the mote that happens to be in their eye.

Sadly, we all have this problem to one degree or another.

One particular person, that comes to mind quite readily, continually complained about the ministry staff in their local assembly. Making accusations that, from the pastor through all the leadership, no one cared about people. All of them were supposedly chasing off people by their uncaring attitudes. Funny thing was, this individual had been responsible for dozens of people leaving and never coming back because of the continual complaining and untimely rants to new converts or in front of people who had never even darkened the door as of yet.

There are some things you have to know before you can begin to cultivate a caring attitude in any group.

Know Your Soil

Before we journey into the working of the ground, it is imperative that we identify two things...

    1) What type of soil do we have?
    2) What is the condition of the soil?

These two areas are fundamental questions to ask and answer before we can begin our plan of action. Once both have been fully understood, then, we move toward actions.

The type of soil will determine the type of seed that can survive, the depth at which you can plant, and the amount of work that will be needed to prepare the soil.

The condition will require one to take a soil sample and send to a specialist to report what chemicals, fertilizer, or crop that will be needed to boost the nutrient levels. Some conditions can be observed by sight or feel, but it takes a deeper analysis to find what is hidden within the soil.

We too have to understand how fertile the base soil would be within the hearts of people to see what is needed to cultivate them further. Some require a limited amount of fertilization while others may require a contract with the neighboring hog farm to bring a LOT of "fertilizer" to just get them started. And, there are some that the only way they will ever be productive again will be if we run a plow through the soil and completely tear it down so that the negative influences can be buried deep enough that they do not germinate and sprout back up.

I saw some of the rockiest ground in France being worked and planted with the same type of crops we have in Midwest United States! Even though it looked like a "rock patch", the farmers were able to produce a crop around those rocks. It reminded me of the plains in South Dakota. It may not produce as much but they were working it and gleaning a harvest, which tells me that just about any soil can be used if cultivated.

Cultivating

I do not use this term because it makes the phrase sound catchy. Rather, it reminds me of a farming process that is so needful to achieve maximum results when harvest time rolls around.

Here are some short definitions for "Cultivating"…

- to loosen or break up the soil
- to improve by labor, care, or study
- to encourage
- to seek the society of

Each definition could be dissected to enhance this thought, but, for the sake of time we will simplify by saying, it takes focused effort for the purpose of seeing specific results.

"Prepare to plan, plan to prepare" would be a great quote to compliment what the process of cultivating desires to achieve. It is an asserted effort to improve, encourage, and enhance the ability to grow. This process cannot be limited to just farming because there are so many areas of life that must be cultivated to maximize a specific experience.

A quick look at the surface can be deceiving. Appearing to be smooth on top, but due to ruts from past years of pushing through mud or running an implement too fast, the subsurface can be flawed, causing erosion problems, moisture issues, or just tearing up equipment.

There are many implements or tools that can be used to cultivate, with the intent of encouraging the soil to produce at a higher quality and quantity; Plows, disks, excelorators, rollers, rippers, field cultivators…and many more. Each have specific uses and purposes that will either open up the ground to allow roots to go deeper, bring moisture to the surface, break down the clods of dirt so that the seed can spring up easily, to smoothing the surface for better planting conditions. All methods have their purpose and each is necessary to encourage maximum results. Again, it takes effort! It takes initiative to say, "I will do this thing!"

I will borrow a phrase from a song my dad wrote many years ago, "Break up your fallow ground…". We are challenged to use wisdom along with initiative to see that souls are saved and lives are mended.

Post harvest is no time to sleep! As long as the weather holds up, the preparations are pushed to continue to prepare the ground for the next season. There is no slack time in cultivating a culture of caring…

Culture of Caring

We live in a fast paced world…just in case you have not noticed. And, the Church has fallen prey to the same mentality as our culture.

We look for the malls and large department stores instead of the locally owned shops downtown. Spending ten dollars gas to save five! Companies grow by gobbling up smaller "mom and pop" shops, causing consolidation and eventual job loss, and pricing escalation for consumers.
Mega churches are the rave. Consolidate, bigger is better,

strength in numbers, no matter how far one needs to drive its convenient to just be fed. So, all the talents from the small community churches are being drawn to the larger stages, creating the attraction of light shows and beautiful voices and bands to accompany. Many feel that they must find the best talent for the worship band to create the ambiance for those that come. An anxiousness is bred into the leadership…a man made anxiety that we will loose our place of recognition if we cannot provide the best experience possible for the parishioners.

What we have lost, in all of this consolidation, is the individual service and personal touch. While the gain is more entertainment, leverage, and buying power.

This phenomenon has left us enjoying the "light show", but void of personal interaction with others who really care. One can slip in and get their fix for the week. Just do your duty for that week and still get to Cracker Barrel before the Sunday crowds.

We are not winning our neighbors because we are so involved with distant "relationships" that do not require so much effort. All of our technology advances and ability to travel quickly to greater distances has given us a new freedom, but it doesn't relieve us of the responsibility for our neighbors. Why talk to someone next door when I can converse with people half way around the world. Besides, it's too much work building relationships that are closer to me. So, we "Tap Out" by having a lot of conversation (chat) and not enough communication (personal).

While our neighbors are crying out for Truth we focus our attention on Skype Services in foreign countries. Instead of going, we have our cake and eat it too by staying home but feeling like we have done our duty by preaching to someone in Pakistan or South Africa.

I'm not opposed to larger churches, using Facebook or Skype, or any other means of sharing the Gospel, so don't get me wrong on this. However, it does present a challenge where we must begin to "Cultivate a Culture of Caring" within the confines of our local congregation, or structure of influences, so that we continue to love our neighbor as our selves. Those within arms length are our first responsibility!

It has been my experience that when our structure is challenged, everyone gets frustrated. Yet, we are not willing to make honest adjustments and changes, resulting in a revolving door and the bodies of those forsaken riddle the trail behind us.

These things should not be!

Power does not come in numbers. Power comes from Yahweh alone! It isn't in light shows, as cool as they are. The resurrecting power of Grace is the only thing that will save. Jesus stated in Matthew 18:20 very clearly what it takes to have His presence, *"For where two or three are gathered together in my name, there am I in the midst of them."* Jesus will be where believers will gather together in love and unity…no matter the number. Seek Him first…before all the fluff, puff, and entertainment stuff.

We need a revival of conscience awareness of those around us. I'm convinced that the church that is aware of souls is a church that is growing. Growth by draining the church down the street is not profiting the Kingdom at all. Only growth by reaching to the lost next door, or under a bridge that we pass each day, or the children in our neighborhood, and teaching those that have been placed in our care, will build up and bring increase to God's World.

The following will illustrate the atrocity of where our society, inside and outside the church, is at today:

The Violinist Test

Perhaps you've read or heard about the Washington Post experiment to determine the reaction and nature of our society to fine music.

In December 2008 they tried an experiment called "A Violinist in the Metro" which involved a man sitting in a Washington DC metro station playing a violin. The violinist played six Bach pieces for approximately 45 minutes on a violin worth 3.5 million dollars.
During the time the violinist played, only a handful of people even stopped to listen out of over one thousand people that

passed him by.

Ironically this violinist was world renowned, Joshua Bell, who would sell out theaters around the world. Just two days before, seats at a Boston theater were sold at an average of $100 each. Just to hear him play the very pieces that people walked by without hardly a glance his way.

The Washington Post concluded from this experiment, *"If we do not have a moment to stop and listen to one of the best musicians in the world playing <u>the best music</u> ever written, how many other things are we missing?"*

How many times have we walked past bruised and hurting people and never recognize the need because of our hurried lifestyle. Schedules, pleasures, and self indulging supersede the tug of the Holy Spirit that attempts to draw our attention to the needs of humanity.

Watch what Jesus boldly declares in John 10:27, *"My sheep hear my voice, and I know them, and they follow me"* If there was ever a day in the history of mankind that we desperately need every Bible thumping Christian to hear the voice of the Great Shepherd, it is in these last hours.

Many speak of knowing the voice of God, but, I for one, will not rest until I have tuned into the frequency that will guide me and direct me to every hungry soul.

No grand standing or embarrassing a waitress or the gas station attendant, but, listening to that still small voice that will lead to the hungry. As Jesus would stay at the well and send everyone else away, so that he could zero in on one woman that had her life wrecked by sin. By focusing His attention directly on her He was able to pull her from the pit.

Speak Lord, we will hear the cry of the hurting and lost around us. We will take our eyes off of the show long enough for the Holy Spirit to guide us to the broken.

The Hurting Are Right Next Door

I recall preaching in Arkansas for a dear friend and as we

reclined in the comfort of his home, he began to share some news of a lady that lived just a few miles from them. As the story unfolded my heart began to pound as I felt the Spirit of God nudging me to listen more intently. I could not get away from it, so, I went online and found the article so that I could share in more detail.

The headline, "Janice Robbins Stabbed Granddaughter, Killed Self". That in it self can bring a tear to one's eye!

As the story unfolded we find a grandmother who was completely distraught after loosing her son. While the people who went to church with her, her neighbors, and those that had saw her last did not have a clue that she was contemplating a suicide murder. She wrote an explanation note, placed a few personal items in a vehicle, then went back into the house and stabbed her granddaughter, set the house on fire and laid down beside the little girl to parish in the flames.

How sad! Not just that such a story could have even happened, but that others were not close enough, or sensitive enough, to recognize that she was struggling.

Yet, we could be living next door to someone just like her.

This article sent shock waves of pain through my soul as I realized how close the hurting are to every one of us. If we do not hear the voice of God we will pass them by, and another will enter eternity without knowing the hope of a loving and caring God.

Remember this…

> *"Too often we underestimate the power of a touch, a smile, a kind word, a listening ear, an honest compliment, or the smallest act of caring, all of which have the potential to turn a life around."*
> ~ *Leo Buscaglia (1925 - 1998)*

God made us to enjoy the personal touch of others. It is one who has built the walls so tight, that no one can penetrate, who becomes miserable with life and others. It's a self inflicted pain that cannot be ignored.

Cultivate a Culture of Caring…it may hurt at times, and it may be a challenge to your personality, but, in some way, find the fortitude to step out and care for someone around you. Don't let the news find you in wonder of how a neighbor, friend, family member, or church family member has given up on life. What a tragedy to know that we could have done something…but didn't.

THE "WHO CARES" SYNDROME

CHAPTER 3

Have you heard that phrase? I recall growing up with two sisters and when all arguments were exhausted, the retort would be "Who Cares?!". Although short, this phrase holds a great amount of power in it. It's not as much the words, although they do hold much relevance, but, more importantly the implied emotion behind the message.

When the phrase "who cares" is used by youngsters, to help draw closure to an argument, it isn't quite as impactful upon one's destiny. But, if this takes root in a child's heart and the root becomes a vine in their youth, it can become detrimental and destructive. When a teen begins to feel that no one cares, the emotional upheaval simply drives them into a state of separation from those that may care, but have not adequately expressed it. This stage in a teenager's life must be continually monitored. We use the terms of "self-esteem" or "self worth" to attempt to bring attention to the "Who Cares" attitude before it takes root in their spirit.

I would attempt to take this into another dimension…that being, when this same question has fallen into the heart of an adult, it is destructive. Depression, disillusionment, separation from all that is good, and suicide can grip the emotions, making them unstable. Whether in their late twenties and struggling with late-life dating, or emotions that come with settling into a marriage, or, in their forties when mid-life begins to ask "Who am I", "What have I done in this life", and "What meaning is there to all that I've gained". Or, even an individual in their golden years feeling left alone without loved ones surrounding them as they had hoped.

In all levels of adulthood the Who Cares Syndrome will destroy the ability to be productive in the Kingdom. It is a "show stopper"! It will kill all creativity and will block the road to purpose, dreams, and vision.

> *The freeway requires that you keep moving, no matter what you witness along the way. Has the same mentality crept into the church?*

14

I declare, through personal experience, that we must be aware of this growing epidemic of the "Who Cares" attitude.

This portion is for those who are currently feeling the painful hurts of isolation, with no one that cares, and, it is for those who have never fell prey to this roaring lion. It is real! It will destroy…but, "Who Cares?"

Does God Care?

Let me provide some assurance from Isaiah 40:1, which says, *"Comfort ye, comfort ye my people, saith your God."*

No matter what the circumstances…even if God is rebuking and bringing discomfort into our lives to see His will performed in us, we can be assured that He is still concerned that we are comforted. And, that we comfort one another.

It is very disheartening to feel used…

The ebb and flow of life will require more or less human touch in a person's life. But, it is better to err on the side of over indulgence than not enough.

The question was asked, "How does a person get to the point where they would say 'I'm not sure that God cares' after being in the church for a long time?" I will attempt to answer this question…in short, it is a lacking of the human touch of caring people.

Truth be told, the question should not be "Does God care?", rather it should be "I don't feel that people care, which gives a negative reflection of the God they claim to represent".

Our response to "Does God care?" should be two fold:

1. God Cares and He has shown us He cares
2. I care and I will show you I care

These two points simply provide the fundamental requirement for securing a person's emotional need for caring.

God cares and what more would He need to do to show us that

He cares. He has already marched up a hill, called Golgotha, going to great lengths to show us how much He cares for us.

The responsibility has been placed in the hands of His followers to allow God to work through us to insure every person is cared for.

It is no surprise that the first order of business brought before the Apostles were concerns about care of the widows (Acts 6:1). It set the course of how the church was to respond to the needs of people. It isn't all about the miracles, signs, and wonders…our calling is to care for those around us.

I Will Come To You!

John 14:18 provides words from Jesus that goes like this *"I will not leave you comfortless: I will come to you."*

The translation, for comfortless, implies "orphans".

An orphan is one deprived of father and mother, neglected, caused to wander about from place to place in hopes of finding a foster family that would take them in until they are old enough to fend for themselves. Stripped of the comforts, support, and direction afforded to a child raised in a stable environment. An orphan will be more susceptible to disease and death due to their lack of love, caring, and general environment.

Jesus says, "I will not leave you as an orphan"! One that is lost and undone and prey for all the predators of this world! I will come to you!

I find it interesting that he says that he will come to us. When did it become the King's responsibility to come to the peasant? What decree proclaimed that Royalty would be required to stoop to the level of the commoner? Isn't it the natural way for the subjects to come and entertain, bow down, and pay obeisance to the Magistrate? Jesus must have gotten his wires crossed somewhere along the way! Why would he have to come to us? We should go to him and beg!

Is it any wonder that Psalms 8:5 and Hebrews 2:7 would provide a vivid picture of how the Messiah isn't some "better than thou" figure that demanded worship. But that God robed Himself in lowly flesh, becoming lower than the angelic forces, appearing in weak humanity, for the purpose of redeeming man to Himself.

God has always come to the aide of mankind, like the young lover that would come to the door with gifts, flowers, and words of flattery for just a chance to court the one he loves. She doesn't have to throw herself at him with lewd or suggestive motives. He stands at the door knocking, with a gentle whisper of "May I come into your life?".

Oh, that we would see this concept through the eyes of God!

Pride Hinders Our Ability To Care

Mark 7:21-23 lists pride as one of the issues that will defile a man. When we become so "heavenly minded that we are of no earthly good" it is a dangerous place to stand. Listed right along with adulteries, fornications, murders, thefts, covetousness, wickedness, deceit, lasciviousness, an evil eye, and blasphemy we find the sin of pride. Each of these issues, as the Scripture calls them, have their root in the heart of a man. We must ask God to pull pride out of our heart by the root so that we can see others through the eyes of love. Notice that every one of these issues are sins against humanity with the exception, perhaps, of blasphemy.

The only way we will truly love people, as God would love them, is to have a change of heart. Pride cannot remain, or it will hinder our ability to care for those who we see as "lower" than us.

Pride blinds to the needs of others. Due to pride's affects, it will make its way onto the list of sins that defile a man. Right along with all those sins that are viewed as evil, yet because of its obscure nature we tend to excuse and over look it.

Pride will keep one from making that first call to someone we have hurt, it will keep us from humility, it will exalt its self and still appear to be humble, Stifling our relationships with others.

Pride kills relationships! It is no wonder it is listed with such sins of the flesh!!

Which Is The Great Commandment?

A lawyer, in his typical way, attempts to cross examine Jesus by asking a question for the purpose of entrapping him into an argument. Matthew 22:36-40 provides the following interchange;

> *"Master, which is the great commandment in the law?*
> *Jesus said unto him, Thou shalt love the Lord thy God with all thy heart, and with all thy soul, and with all thy mind. This is the first and great commandment.*
> *And the second is like unto it, Thou shalt love thy neighbour as thyself. On these two commandments hang all the law and the prophets."*

Jesus first establishes a well known fact for all that stood close by, that the greatest commandment was that you love the Lord thy God with all thy heart, soul, and mind. This was no great revelation to these good Jews, for this was fundamental to all of their teaching! How could anyone answer otherwise? So, Jesus starts with the obvious…as He usually does…and affirmed that which had been passed down from generation to generation…which was, God first!

The interesting thing in this passage was not only that we should love Elohim with all our heart, soul, and mind. Nor was it really that he indicates that we should love our neighbor as our selves. This too is a commandment, right?

Let's look at two points…

The first point would be in Jesus' statement that "the second is 'like unto' it". Like unto what? Jesus equated the second commandment to the first, and went as far as to say, in simple terms, that you are to love your neighbor with all your heart, soul, and mind…like unto…in the same manner that you love the Lord your God! Wait a minute, we might say…hold your horses, we can't put humanity on the same level as Deity! The discussion isn't about which is more important or which has

18

more power, or which would be deserving of all honor, glory, and worship. That would be a no brainer! Jehovah is the only One that would be on that level, but, the point that I would submit to you would be that Jesus is telling us that we must love our neighbor or we will never be able to love God. How can you love God whom you have not seen if you cannot love your neighbor that you have seen?

The second point that stands out in this passage is the "neighbor". We find that the Greek word *plēsion* (play-see'-on) is used and it is a derivative of the word pelas, which is interpreted as "near". Anything or anyone, at any point in time that is "near", is the basic meaning of this word. So, if I am on an airplane my neighbor is on the plane with me! If I am walking down the street I must be conscience of the fact that those walking or sitting along the way are near, thereby classified as my neighbor. In a bit broader sense it can also mean the fellow Christians, or those that I go to church with, or professing Christians down the street. If we broaden it a little further the word *plesion* can also mean fellow countryman…someone that has a similar origin by location. That being anyone from my town, county, state, or country in which I live. This broad sweep of the brush will capture just about anyone that would come my way.

With these two points in mind, I believe that Jesus was telling the lawyer that we must love humanity or we will never love God. Our depth of concern for humanity will determine the depth of concern about God and what He desires. If we cannot love that which God loves, then we cannot claim to love God, for His creation has His complete attention and love.

If we do not embrace humanity, we cannot embrace God. If we cannot weep for the created, we will never weep for the Creator. If we have no feelings toward all mankind (my neighbor) then we cannot have truthful feelings toward God. Without a love for our neighbor then it is a sounding brass and tinkling symbol in God's eyes.

Who Is "My Neighbor"?

Once Jesus has focused the spot light on dealing with our neighbor this "certain lawyer" began to feel the heat of conviction and this brought to him a need to justify himself. Isn't it interesting how natural this reaction is for us all? Jesus certainly did not let up. He picked up a few sticks and added to the fire to turn up the heat a little more!

When ask, "Who is my neighbor?", Jesus gave a very familiar parable that many a sermon has dissected, using it for illustrations to prove many points. Many of which could be applicable, but, I believe the Lord directed me to the reason for the parable in the first place.

It wasn't just about those who stopped to help or didn't. Nor was it entirely about a man falling among thieves and another showing kindness to him.

Keep in mind that the context is that the Lawyer is asking the question, "Who is my neighbor", and Jesus is responding to his inquiry. Also remember that "neighbor" can be interpreted as anyone that is close in proximity at any given time, a countryman, or one that becomes our comrade or companion. Jesus is honing in on the fact that we must be a neighbor to all that we come in contact with. In fact, due to the example of our Lord, it has become our commandment to do the same as our example. To walk across the road and reach into a ditch of miry sin and pull folks out of their situations, carry them to a place to be tended to, even if it costs us all!

Where did we get the pious idea that it isn't our responsibility?

Oh, that's right, it wasn't the religious that stopped, in this parable, either! It is no wonder that the religious leaders didn't like Jesus…he didn't ask to come to their homes for supper. He went to the publicans and sinners homes for dinner.

If I may, I will bring this to a clear message without any smoke screens. Jesus responded to the question of "who is my neighbor" by sending this message to all that would hear it in the future. He came to be bruised for our iniquities, and he was both the bruised and the one that came to heal the bruised. And, in like manner, he is admonishing us to follow his example and always look to the gutter to find a brother that has fallen prey and may be laying there with the life's blood pouring out of him. Perhaps, you are the one that has been crushed and are now in need of a "neighbor" that will reach to you.

Don't Just See The Need

> *1 John 4:20-21*, *"If a man say, I love God, and hateth his brother, he is a liar: for he that loveth not his brother whom he hath seen, how can he love God whom he hath not seen? And this commandment have we from him, That he who loveth God love his brother also."*

DON'T GO THERE...DON'T EVEN START TO ASK WHO'S MY BROTHER!

That would sound a lot like, "Who's my neighbor?"…

It is easier to love something you've not had to live with! Ask anyone that has been married for a number of years. To say you love God is to say that you love what God loves…your brother…your neighbor…anyone that you have to deal with in the flesh.

To hate (strongly dislike or despise) a human while declaring that you love God is a direct rejection of God's commandments. Love the person and hate the sin…but don't let it get confused.

Without becoming judgmental one can identify the sin in a person's life, and attempt to help them address it. But, to allow the sin to separate, or cause to despise their existence, then we have allowed the sin to skew our vision. Let the love of God recapture our heart, that it can flow through us, even when we can't in our own human nature.

Who Cares Syndrome

Many are asking, "Who Cares?" and it is now taking root in our belief system to the point that doctrine doesn't matter because those that are strong do not bear the infirmities of those who have become weakened by the thoughts of "Who cares about me?"

Sadly, I must confess that I have been on both sides of this fence, which is why I have become more adamant about seeing this message take hold. I have been strong in mind, spirit, and body…until loosing sight of those that are weak.

The call is for us to cultivate, break up some fallow ground, and sow the seeds of caring about every soul around us. Satan is the accuser, and we must stand against his wily ways of making accusations. Satan is the abuser, so, we must become the encouragers that pour the salve into the wounds. Counter attacks must be made until we have nurtured and cultivated a culture in our home, church, and communities that show the spirit of consolation to all around us. It does take time to care…is it worth the most precious commodity of all? If not, then perhaps we have self-indictments all around us.

Who Cares?!

"Cultivate a Culture of Caring". Jesus cared and it took Him to a cross. How far would you go? The old adage is so true, "People don't care what you know until they know that you care". If we will grasp this concept and get it in our spirit, we will win our "world".

Welles Crowther – "The Man in the Red Bandana"

Have you heard the story of Welles Crowther?

Welles lost his life in the 9-11 attacks on the World Trade Centers in New York City in 2001. A young man who worked as an equities trader, but will be remembered by many as the one who single handedly saved dozens of lives, yet giving his life in the final collapse of the towers.

Recognized by the red bandana that he had with him at all times, Welles went multiple times back into the smoky confines of the tower to guide or physically carry people down the stairs to safety. Accounts began to surface as his parents continued to piece together his last moments of his life. People that he didn't know are alive today because he loved to help people. People of all color…creed didn't matter…status or title wasn't important. He just kept going back in for human beings!

Oh that we could catch just a taste of what Welles Crowther had in his heart…better yet, if we could get a dosage of what our Heavenly Father thinks about Humanity.

Who is my neighbor?

Confession Is Good For The Soul

I'll never forget that Sunday afternoon when an acquaintance stopped by my home and began to weep as he asked, "Have I done anything wrong to you?" It was a humbling moment, as we reflected back over six years, but that wasn't the most humbling for me.

As we continued our conversation that afternoon, he began to share with me that when he walked away from God, and the church body, there were only a couple of people that actually continued to reach out to him. I was not one of them. He didn't come to condemn me, but, as we talked about all that had transpired, it kept going through my mind how that I had been too busy "doing the Lord's work" to make one phone call, email, text, or personal visit to this young man.

I know that there are billions of souls on this earth and it is impossible to touch them all. As a matter of fact, without the absolute power of God, it is virtually impossible to reach the community that we live in. But, we cannot use the millions as an excuse to not reach to those that we can.

He Cares – I Care

When You Truly Feel That No One Cares
And The Load You Carry Is So Hard To Bear
Just Remember That Jesus Is Always There

When You Think You've Reached Your End...
And No One Left To Call Your Friend
Just Remember, On Jesus You Can Depend

When You Feel That All Hope Is Gone
And All Your Nights Are So Very Long
Just Remember That Jesus Gives The Song

When You've Cried Both Night And Day
And You've Seemed To Have Lost Your Way
Just Remember To Take Time To Pray

Never Give Up Just Hold To His Hand
Even When All Seems To Be Sinking Sand
You Are Part Of His Master Plan

By Joseph Atkins

I picked this poem up from the author and felt it an appropriate reminder that no matter what the circumstances Jesus is there to see us through. Though others fail, and we all will, our Savior will find the one sheep and bring comfort to their wounded soul. Jesus cared for every soul, we too must pick up the cross and carry the burden for every soul.

Yes! Every soul does count with God. And, He Cares about You!

A CALL FOR SONS OF CONSOLATION

CHAPTER 4

The Book of Acts has many prominent characters that did some mighty exploits through the power of the Holy Ghost. Peter preached the first sermon at the first Apostolic convention! Stephen was stoned for the Gospel. Paul is struck down, converted, and preached the Gospel further than any other of the early church forefathers. Nestled into all these great men and women we find one man who arguably is the most important figure in the first century church age. This man is Joses, surnamed Barnabas.

I am intrigued by Barnabas. Where would the early church be without him? What about Paul? Would Paul's ministry have been as powerful as it was if Barnabas had not been there? What about others…would they have been as successful or would they have gone to places such as northern Africa to start powerful works that contended for the Gospel of Jesus Christ for centuries to follow? Where would they have been without a Barnabas who encouraged and supported them?

While Acts chapter four gives us the first glimpse of Barnabas, his presence is noted throughout the New Testament church.

Take note that Barnabas was not his birth name. Joses was "surnamed" Barnabas because he had a track record of being a man of consolation. Meaning, encourager. He was the first to reach out to Saul (Paul), without fear of his past life, after his conversion.

Barnabas examples a man without fear, willing to take a risk when he felt compelled, soft hearted enough to go the extra mile to reach to the outcast, and was willing to "play second fiddle" to see the Gospel furthered.

Some believed that Barnabas was a large man that was less inclined to speak. This opinion is drawn from Acts 14:12 when Barnabas was called Jupiter and Paul Mercurius. Jupiter being the "father of the gods", and Mercurius is god of eloquence and the messenger and attendant of Jupiter, in the heathen mythology. With this in mind, Barnabas must have been envisioned as the leader and Paul as the mouthpiece for him.

Oh how we need the spirit of Barnabas in our midst! What talents have we lost because we had too few "sons of consolation"? How many have fallen to the wayside because too few have picked up the spiritual banner of becoming a "son of consolation"?

I would move our attention now to John Mark, who traveled with Paul and Barnabas on their first "missions" trip. Partially through the journey he became home sick and went home. Paul had this brash attitude that John Mark was a "momma's boy".

When the next tour was to begin Paul refused to take him along. Barnabas and Paul strongly disagreed. Acts 15:29 spells it out like this, "..*the contention was so sharp between them, that they departed asunder one from the other*". Barnabas separated himself from Paul to go with John Mark and be the "encourager" to him, while Paul selected Silas for his travel companion.

Thank God for a Barnabas that will have an encouraging spirit to the point that they will stand against the establishment so that restoration could be accomplished.

The "son of encouragement". What a powerful title! A title given that was not requested, only deserved due to the life that Joses lived.

Where are the Barnabas' today? We do have examples, but too few and far between.

Where Does Consolation Begin?

So glad you ask! Consolation begins in the fulfillment of our relationship with Jesus Christ and His acceptance of us into "the glory of God". When in the flow, the attitude of encouragement begins in the fact that God has received us and we, in response to God's grace, respond by allowing the same acceptance flow out of us to others. When a body of believers become too alike they have missed this concept entirely. If the group becomes too white, black, latino, rich, or any other segregation of "likeness"…when you've seen one, you've seen 'em all…cookie cutter Christians…then we have begun to lack in consolation.

Let us examine **Romans 15:1-7** for some guidance on this subject,

> *"We then that are strong ought to bear the infirmities of the weak, and not to please ourselves. Let every one of us please his neighbour for his good to edification. For even Christ pleased not himself; but, as it is written, The reproaches of them that reproached thee fell on me. For whatsoever things were written aforetime were written for our learning, that we through patience and comfort of the scriptures might have hope. Now the God of patience and consolation grant you to be likeminded one toward another according to Christ Jesus: That ye may with one mind and one mouth glorify God, even the Father of our Lord Jesus Christ. Wherefore receive ye one another, as Christ also received us to the glory of God."*

What an admonishment! It is the concept of strong bearing up the weak.

The one thing that I have observed, in my years of connecting with various groups of believers, with many varying degrees of rules and beliefs, is that all will walk through a valley at some point in their life.

The ability to humble ourselves and admit that we are human, and that failure is just as possible in my life as it is with the drunkard, is not the norm. Yet, so many will pretend to be above failure to the point that even if they tell a lie that it is justified in their mind because…well…they are above failure.

Blessed are the merciful, for they shall find mercy. This kind of attitude only comes through a life of hard knocks and realization that I'm vulnerable and prone to the same human nature as the next guy. Too many, especially in leadership, have felt the pressure to perform so heavy that it has become a front to act as though they can't fail. Truthful leadership will be the first to step in front of a crowd or congregation and say "I'm sorry".

Just as Christ did not seek to please himself but suffered for us all, we too are admonished to seek to "please" our neighbor and not our own selves. If we lived this simple message, oh what would our witness be like? I'm convinced that the lost would see our good works and desire to know what causes such selfless giving of ourselves to others.

We have fallen far short of what God has desired for His Church to be. Sure, salvation of every soul is His primary concern, but, interwoven into the same fabric it is His will that we love our fellow man.

Philippians 2:1-4 lays out God's intentions for Christ's coming into this earth…

> *"If there be therefore any* **consolation in Christ***, if any comfort of love, if any fellowship of the Spirit, if any bowels and mercies, Fulfill ye my joy, that ye be likeminded, having the same love, being of one accord, of one mind. Let nothing be done through strife or vain glory; but in lowliness of mind let each esteem other better than themselves. Look not every man on his own things, but every man also on the things of others."*

Note that the word "consolation" is being used in verse one. If there be any encouragement in Christ…look out for one another!

Again, my intention is not to say that salvation and heaven are secondary, but, it is God's will that we do all things to "esteem other better than themselves".

When Paul says to the Philippian church, *"Look not every man on his own things, but every man also on the things of others"* his intent is not for us to covet our neighbor's car, but rather that, we are concerned about the needs of others before our own needs.

This is true Christianity…true Christ-likeness…to place the needs of others before our own desires!

Remember, James 1:27 says this*, "Pure religion and undefiled before God and the Father is this, To visit the fatherless and widows in their affliction, and to keep himself unspotted from the world."*

Encourager Defined

1. To inspire with hope, courage, or confidence.
2. To give support to; foster
3. To stimulate; spur: (*burning the field to encourage new plant growth.*)

A negative person or leader will always find the need to induce fear tactics to motivate people...encouragers induce praise tactics!

Encore! Encore! Encore!!

Just as a performer longs to hear the applause of the crowd, and the cry of "Encore" at the end of a performance or concert, most people work harder when a timely applause lifts them to give one more demonstration of excellence!

An encore is defined as...

1. A demand by an audience for an additional performance, usually expressed by applause.
2. An additional performance in response to the demand of an audience.

The applause and obvious satisfaction by those in the crowd will cause the actors to come out for another bow, a singer to sing one more song, a baseball player to step back out of the dugout and give a tip of the cap. With no hesitation, they will go the extra mile to please those in attendance.

The unfortunate truth is that it is a human trait to tear down before we build up others. It is patronizing when you encourage upward and fail to encourage downward. It also shows our true heart of feeling superior to others.

I will never tell someone they can't! I may help them see obstacles or challenges, but, through Christ Jesus they can do all things! Think as big as your faith will take you!!

Clap your hands and clap more! Use positive reinforcement more! Listen more! Keep in mind that your ego system is just as fragile as theirs, and you are not any bigger if you do not give an encore. Remember that we are all made of the same thing…dirt…from the dust of the earth we were fearfully and wonderfully made.

When the Encourager is Missing

David Huff has a song where it states, "Everybody's got a story to tell…"

Every person has hurts, shattered dreams, and obstacles that had to be overcome. The encourager is needed to bring balance to a world that desires to crush dreams and rip apart lives and hearts of people.

What do we do when the encouragers are missing?

All it takes for a future doctor or lawyer to drop out and look for ways to cope with the painful memories is for someone to say, "You can't…" or "She's not cut out for…." One moment in time that catches the winds of discouragement and the course of life is sent into the Bermuda Triangle.

The countless masses have fell short of goals and dreams because someone very important in their lives buried a stake in the ground and chained them there with discouraging words.

When the encouragers are missing, life happens…and we all loose another valuable piece to the social web that binds us all together.

Appropriate Encouraging Words:

- "I appreciate you ."
- "I love you."
- "I care."
- "I understand."
- "What can I do to help?"

So many people rarely, if ever, hear these words, "I appreciate you." and even fewer hear the words, "I love you.".

Appreciation of someone does not mean you appreciate what they are doing but what they are.

In the absence of these words, many people feel unappreciated, devalued, and taken for granted.

Our responsibility as born again believers is to communicate value, worth, and genuine appreciation that will spark a sense of "Can Do" and spurs further positive growth and action.

Change The World By Encouraging

Its in those moments when you receive a note, card, letter, call, email, or text and the other person says something like…"You were on my heart and I just felt to let you know how much you mean to me."…and our outlook on life makes a u-turn to the better.

It's the combination of those life changing moments that will sustain us at times. The impartation of strength through encouragement will always bring paybacks.

> *Romans 16:1-2, "I commend unto you Phebe our sister, which is **a servant of the church** which is at Cenchrea: That ye receive her in the Lord, as becometh saints, and that ye assist her in whatsoever business she hath need of you: for **she hath been a succourer of many**, and of myself also.*

Phebe is given the key to the city by the Apostle Paul, because of her servant spirit to all and she has been one given to help and strengthen others.

Remember this…

> *Mark 9:41, "For whosoever shall give you a cup of water to drink in my name, because ye belong to Christ, verily I say unto you, he shall not lose his reward."*

Encouragement will change your world with eternal rewards to show for it!

The smallest of efforts will bring dividends in the world to come.

31

As a child of God others will bless you and be rewarded for their blessings on your behalf.

Give and it shall be given unto you pressed down, shaken together, and running over shall men give unto you! That is a promise that comes from the bowels of first giving of our selves to the kingdom.

Encourage…Be Encouraged!

Let God choose for you, it will be the right decision.
Let God guide you, it will be the right direction.
Let God plan for you, it will be in the right timing.
Let God measure for you, it will be the right portion.
Let God help you, it will be the right care.
Let God instruct you, it will be the right teaching.
Let God train you, it will be the right preparation.
Let God counsel you, it will be the right perspective.
Let God fight for you, it will be the right outcome.
Let God work with you, it will be the right result!

Why Care?

I have a close friend that has been faithful to God and man. He and his sweet wife have stood for Truth and Righteousness. Yet, when she found that she had cancer most people distanced themselves which seemed that they forsook them. Not that they didn't care. It was just that so many didn't know what to say, so they simply stayed away. I'm sure many prayed out of feelings of pity. Then came a point where this good man walked out to his back yard, fell on his knees, and ask "Where are you Lord? Who cares, Lord? Lord, I know you can do all things but I feel alone and that my prayers are not being heard!" The prayer was much more in depth than this, but it was a summary of his inner struggle. As we talked he said it just felt that he was alone. And, in tears he expressed his concern that God may be unpleased with his lack of faith. I felt so compelled to help this brother!

The Holy Spirit whispered into my ear to let him know that the true test of faith is not when we feel God and hear his voice but rather when we do not hear anything and yet we believe that He exists and will hear us when we cry out to Him. I am so thankful that I could be there to encourage my friend in his time of doubt.

"Divide and conquer!" is the number one strategy of war. Cut off supplies, starvation will bring self destruction, and eventual submission of will to the enemy.

The reason we need to cultivate a culture of caring is that we have people all around us, even ourselves at times, who have found themselves in the same predicament as my friend.

So, why care?

The Sin of Omission

I recall a great uncle coming to place a rose on my grandfather's casket after many years of holding a grudge and not speaking or forgiving. It is the holding the good act of kindness or the encouraging word for a few moments too long and once it is too late the guilt settles in. I remember as a young man thinking how foolish the act was…the one that would have enjoyed it the most was now gone on and the one left is dealing with the guilt of omission.

Do not let it be said that you waited until a loved one, neighbor, co-worker, friend, or even an acquaintance has passed from this life before we made an attempt to show kindness.

Good Works

The potentials for ministry are endless, in that, it is based on the needs present. The individual that remains flexible, pliable, and sensitive to the Spirit, and to those in need, will find a place to minister to others.

What sets a Mother Theresa apart from all others of the same faith, gender, and profession? It is an unseen force that compels the Christ-like to hone in on a need, like a laser guided missile. Compassion begins to spark in the soul as the heart melts and the mind rushes to understand and prepare the way for compassion to be released into the broken lives.

Most of us struggle with "doing good", which is a bi-product of compassion.

What is "good"? And, what is "good works? We can never merit heaven based on our goodness or righteous living. It is never a matter of how much "good" can we do to muster up enough points to pass the "holy course" and graduate to the other side. This sin nature has contaminated every fiber of our existence. And without the Grace of God we would never become a "good Johnny".

Matthew 19:17 explains that *"…there is none good but one, that is, God…"* so we might as well leave that futile attempt alone.

Scripture is very clear, on the other hand, that "Good Works" is a bi-product of faith working in us…The goodness of God working through us.

> *James 2:17, "Even so faith, if it hath not works, is dead, being alone."*

There is a natural flow from "faith" to "good works". It just happens!

Scripture does reference good works in several places…let's take a quick glance:

- *Acts 9:36 – "full of good works"*
- *1 Timothy 2:9,10 – "Adorned with good works"*
- *1 Timothy 6:18 – "rich in good works"*
- *Titus 2:7 – admonished to have a "pattern of good works"*
- *Titus 2:14 – we are to be "zealous of good works"*
- *Titus 3:8 – be "careful to maintain good works"*
- *Hebrews 10:24 – we should "provoke unto…good works"*

Our quick conclusion is that good works are admonished, while attempting to be good is not obtainable without the power of the Holy Spirit and forgiving blood of Christ Jesus.

The majority of us look at Scripture and begin to pursue good by doing good things. We clean up the outside, polish up our vocabulary, cut out all the forbidden deeds of drugs, alcohol, pornography, and promiscuous ways, and we throw ourselves into a career path or new vocation within the church to "be good". We ask ourselves, "Well, doesn't the Bible tell us that we are to take up our cross and follow Jesus? This job is my cross." Yet, we miss the real focus that Jesus exampled to us.

Do good because you are forgiven and being transformed into His likeness, but don't try and be good...you'll fail and live in constant doubt of your salvation if you only try to be good. Accept the grace and mercy of God, through Christ Jesus our Lord, and move on to doing good things for those around you.

The Force That Moves - Compassion

Jesus left us an example of the one ingredient that really moves mountains! There seems to be a connection in the Spirit realm with our emotional connection to a need.

You see what your eyes are trained to look for...

I recall working for a friend who had a car crushing business. We would go into junk yards and clean out any vehicles that had been stripped down to the point that they needed to get them out of the way.

We would also drive along the highway and if we saw a couple of cars sitting out in a field, we'd stop and check to see if they wanted to get them out of the way. When I first started helping I remember Paul pointing at a half dozen cars sitting back in the woods or out in a field with weeds covering them and I would have passed them by without ever noticing them. As time went on, my senses began to sharpen and I would anticipate finding them, instead of an after thought.

The same can be applied to going mushroom hunting. When you get into the "zone" it seems that they are popping up everywhere. But, there are days when I could trip over a moral and still not see it. It is about becoming aware.

Compassion is an ingredient that sharpens our senses and makes us painfully aware of a need, and catapults our conscience mind into the realm of what the Spirit can and will do. It's like the baseball player that can't see the ball spinning toward him at 90 miles an hour until his reflexes begin to get into a flow and then the ball seems to slow down, giving him the ability to focus on that little object called a baseball.

Compassion will get us into the zone. When we are confronted with a need, it slows down our speeding mental state and allows us to focus on a single need. It blocks out the crowd and all other distractions…the need becomes the most important thing at that given moment. It connects us in such a way that faith will become the reflexes, and will summons the Holy Spirit to do its work!

Notice how this works with Jesus…

> *Matthew 14:14*, *"And Jesus went forth, and saw a great multitude, and was **moved with compassion** toward them, and he healed their sick."*

> *Mark 1:40-41*, *"And there came a leper…And Jesus, **moved with compassion**, put forth his hand, and <u>touched him</u>, and saith unto him, 'I will; be thou clean'"*

> *Matthew 15:32*, *"Then Jesus called his disciples unto him, and said, '**I have compassion on the multitude**…I will not send them away fasting, lest they faint in the way'"*

> *Luke 7:13*, *"And when the Lord saw her, he **had compassion on her**, and said unto her, 'Weep not'".*

Can you see the trend? Compassion seemed to precede the fulfilling of the need. Compassion seems to allow Jesus to zero in on a single need instead of looking at the masses.

Let's look at some of the parables…

> *Matthew 18:27*, *"Then the lord of that servant was **moved with compassion**, and loosed him, and forgave him the debt."*
> *Luke 10:33*, *"But when a <u>certain</u> Samaritan, as he journeyed, came where he was; and when he saw him, he **had compassion on him**"*

> **Luke 15:20**, *"And he arose, and came to his father. But when he was yet a great way off, his father saw him, and **had compassion**, and ran, and fell on his neck, and kissed him."*

The American College dictionary defines compassion in this way, *"Deep awareness of the suffering of another coupled with the wish to relieve it"*

> **1 Peter 3:8-9**, *"Finally, be ye all of one mind, having compassion one of another, love as brethren, be pitiful, be courteous: Not rendering evil for evil, or railing for railing: but contrarwise blessing; knowing that ye are thereunto called, that ye should inherit a blessing."*

Be determined to make a difference…compassion will bring you to the need and give you the strength to make the difference in someone's life.

> **Jude 17-22**, *"But, beloved, remember ye the words which were spoken before of the apostles of our Lord Jesus Christ; How that they told you there should be mockers in the last time, who should walk after their own ungodly lusts. These be they who separate themselves, sensual, having not the Spirit. But ye, beloved, building up yourselves on your most holy faith, praying in the Holy Ghost. Keep yourselves in the love of God, looking for the Mercy of our Lord Jesus Christ unto eternal life. And of some **have compassion, making a difference**:"*

Compassion will motivate you to make a difference in someone's life!

Are You A Hireling?

John 10:11-13 gives us a perspective that must be considered as we delve further into this never ending subject. In this passage, John speaks of the difference between the "good shepherd" and the "hireling". When all is well, both will stay with the sheep and it becomes hard to distinguish between the two. But, let the wolf come calling and it doesn't take long to identify which one has the most invested in the herd. The hireling will look out for "el numero uno" while the shepherd will risk his very life to save a single sheep.

We have souls dying all around us while we continue to stand on the sidelines and take bets on who will win the battle. It's a dog fight mentality when we are not quite engaged yet pointing to someone in the fight and saying "sick 'em"! Like a spectator at a boxing match that will say, as he leaves the arena, "didn't we do great!". What did "we" do?

Again, I emphasize, it is not for us to "fix" them or their issue, but it is our responsibility to go to them and take them to someone that can nurture them.

In The Mean Time...

Until that day comes, here is what we are admonished to do...

> *Hebrews 10:24-25,* " *Let us hold fast the profession of our faith without wavering; (for he is faithful that promised;) And let us consider one another to* **provoke unto love and to good works***: Not forsaking the assembling of ourselves together, as the manner of some is; but exhorting one another: and so much the more, as ye see the day approaching."*

If I Can Stop One Heart From Breaking by Emily Dickinson

> *If I can stop one heart from breaking,*
> *I shall not live in vain;*
> *If I can ease one life the aching,*
> *Or cool one pain,*
> *Or help one fainting robin*
> *Unto his nest again,*
> *I shall not live in vain.*

There in lies some of the reasons we care! To bear up and lighten the load of one that is hurting.

CHAPTER 6

Remember the words of this old hymn?

> *I was sinking deep in sin, far from the peaceful shore,*
> *Very deeply stained within, sinking to rise no more,*
> *But the Master of the sea, heard my despairing cry,*
> *From the waters lifted me, now safe am I.*
>
> *Love lifted me! Love lifted me!*
> *When nothing else could help*
> *Love lifted me!*
>
> *All my heart to Him I give, ever to Him I'll cling*
> *In His blessed presence live, ever His praises sing,*
> *Love so mighty and so true, merits my soul's best songs,*
> *Faithful, loving service too, to Him belongs.*
>
> *Souls in danger look above, Jesus completely saves,*
> *He will lift you by His love, out of the angry waves.*
> *He's the Master of the sea, billows His will obey,*
> *He your Savior wants to be, be saved today.*

I am continually reminded that the first thing I must remember, when it is difficult to love an individual for any reason, that Jesus loved me. He is my example. Through His actions of love, when I was not lovable or deserving of His gift of love, love absolutely lifted me! When nothing else would help, His love lifted me from the depths of pain and misery. For this, I am thankful and am willing to love those that have done wrongfully.

The Book of John quotes Jesus four times in saying "Love one another"! How can we love if we do not care? How can we fulfill this command when so many are struggling with the thought of "Who Cares"? When the ministry feels alienated and alone and the laity is bogged down with separation. It behooves us to wrestle with this need of loving one another by caring for one another.

Love? What is that?

> **Proverbs 17:17**, *"A friend loveth at all times, and a brother is born for adversity."*

The combination of "loveth at all times" and "born for adversity" depicts how the Holy Spirit would desire to work through us. Always loving and ready to go to the assistance of one that is being bombarded by adversity. That is what a brother does. ".

Trials and tribulations bombard our life and we tend to crawl into the cave and hiss at anything that tries to get into our space. But the love of Christ compels us to walk back out, brush off the dust, and get back into the good fight of faith. Why? Because it isn't just a friend that we are defending, its my brother. And, my new birth has given me the responsibility for him.

I Corinthians 13:1-8 gives the best explanation for love. The King James Version calls it "charity", which is love.

> *"Though I speak with the tongues of men and of angels, and have not charity, I am become as sounding brass, or a tinkling cymbal. And though I have the gift of prophecy, and understand all mysteries, and all knowledge; and though I have all faith, so that I could remove mountains, and have not charity, I am nothing. And though I bestow all my goods to feed the poor, and though I give my body to be burned, and have not charity, it profiteth me nothing. Charity suffereth long, and is kind; charity envieth not; charity vaunteth not itself, is not puffed up, Doth not behave itself unseemly, seeketh not her own, is not easily provoked, thinketh no evil; Rejoiceth not in iniquity, but rejoiceth in the truth; Beareth all things, believeth all things, hopeth all things, endureth all things. Charity never faileth: but whether there be prophecies, they shall fail; whether there be tongues, they shall cease; whether there be knowledge, it shall vanish away."*

This one always nails us! When we hear someone say, "But, I don't love them any more…" Shazam! That's because we do not view that person through the eyes of Godly love. I'm guilty of failing to live up to this Scripture as much as anyone…but it

41

doesn't excuse me from doing what God has instructed me to do.

Love allows others to retain their integrity and dignity, even when they do not deserve it.

A Root of Love

What an amazing little word, "Love". It has been used, misused, and abused in so many ways. It is mentioned 311 times in all scripture, with various applications and levels of meaning. From loving the world to, the opposite end of the spectrum of loving God. From our love for God, to His love for us.

The top users, in Scripture, of the word "love" may not be a surprise to most. Yet, I was quite surprised to find out which book of the Bible uses this term the most.

1 John uses the word "love" thirty three times!

This came as a surprise to me. A little book, yet it shows how John was serious about the fact that love should continue in the Church.

It would be an exhaustive study to examine every single scripture that contained the word "love", but, I do believe we can explore the concepts by boiling down all the verses into a few highlighted points.

I John 3:1-19 uses the following phrases…"*what manner of love the Father hath bestowed upon us… we shall be like him…For this is the message that ye heard from the beginning, that we should love one another…We know that we have passed from death unto life, because we love the brethren. He that loveth not his brother abideth in death. Whosoever hateth his brother is a murderer: and ye know that no murderer hath eternal life abiding in him. Hereby perceive we the love of God, because he laid down his life for us: and we ought to lay down our lives for the brethren. whoso hath this world's good, and seeth his brother have need, and shutteth up his bowels of compassion from him, how dwelleth the love of God in him… let us not love in word, neither in tongue; but in deed and in truth…*"

Ok…shall we sing, "I am a friend of God. I am a friend of

God…" Really? Are you sure?!

We know that we have passed from death unto life because we love the brethren!

Love is a Verb

DC Talk sang a song with a line in it that goes something like this, "Love. Love is a verb…"

Though the vocabulary is a little different for some, the message couldn't be any better. If Christ Jesus our Lord laid down his life for us, when we were unlovable, then why shouldn't we make every attempt to cut some slack for those who disagree with our way and Theology?

Love is a verb…meaning, it is action. It needs traction. No need for factions…ok, I'm not a rap artist by any stretch of imagination, but, if we are going to claim to love, then lets show it with actions. Lip service never expressed love.

No amount of saying "I love you Man!" will ever convince someone, unless there is some kind of sacrificial expression of one's feelings.

If you love your brother what good are you?

Tough Love To Swallow

Jesus, in *Matthew 5:43-48*, takes this "love" thing to a level that boggles the human way of thinking, by saying…

> *"Ye have heard that it hath been said, Thou shalt love thy neighbour, and hate thine enemy. But I say unto you, Love your enemies, bless them that curse you, do good to them that hate you, and pray for them which despitefully use you, and persecute you; That ye may be the children of your Father which is in heaven: for he maketh his sun to rise on the evil and on the good, and sendeth rain on the just and on the unjust. For if ye love them which love you, what reward have ye? do not even the publicans the same? And if ye salute your brethren only, what do ye more than others? do not even the*

publicans so? Be ye therefore perfect, even as your Father which is in heaven is perfect."

I would like to meet the individual that lives this passage. Oh that I could have the mind of Christ at all times, 24/7, every waking moment of each day! Many seem to think that it means to live it on Sunday only.

Jesus points out that a lousy, good for nothing, thieving publican (I may have added something there) can love those that love him.

A publican can walk into Walmart and when an old class mate walks by and says "Howdy", even he can respond with at least a grunt. So how can we think ourselves so wonderful if that's all the love we can muster up?

Our Heavenly Father will cause the sun to rise, and send the rain, not in spite of but for the benefit of, the unjust and the just. No special treatment or a "step child" mentality given to either group.

God's love is extended to all, no matter who they are, what they've done, where they are from, or where they are going. He loves us all without reservation!

To remain on the road toward perfection our love must be stretched to not only be nice to everyone. The admonishment is for us to bless, do good, and pray for those that curse you, hate you, despitefully use or even persecute you.

Seems a little extreme doesn't it? A little over the top, or far fetched! I don't mind that "turn the other cheek" religion, because I can limit how many times I turn the cheek. But to bless someone that has just cussed me out! Now that is simply ludicrous!!

Now we have to deal with all the "what if's…" that come along with logic. What if they kill me? What if they take what I've worked for? What if they have offended me…?

I'm with you…this teaching blows my mind! I need the Holy Spirit in my life to help me with this one.

Love Has No Debt

> **Romans 13:8**, *"Owe no man any thing, but to love one another: for he that loveth another hath fulfilled the law."*

In the preceding verses the apostle is showing the usual protocol for civil magistrates. Duty, reverence, and obedience are to be given to those in authority. No matter what the office our responsibility, as Christians, we are to be in subjection, and to give honor to the place of authority. In other words…Owe no man! Don't withhold anything from those that have rule over you.

On the other hand, owe to your fellow brethren nothing but mutual love. Not being bound in obedience to your brother as you would to the civil authorities, but, love would compel to be a servant to all. Not merely in fear of punishment, but rather by the law of love. It would thrust one into going the extra mile to insure your brother is preferred. Love utterly prevents you from doing anything by which a brother may sustain any kind of injury.

"Acquit yourselves of all obligations except love, which is a debt that must remain ever due" as one rendering put it.

The fulfillment of the law is when love meets action. No longer a matter of duty, but the law now rests in the heart of emotion, affecting the actions. Going beyond the letter of the law and finding its way into the very spirit of mankind.

No longer a debtor to any…but to love unconditionally.

Love is the Pinnacle

II Peter 1:4-9 provides us a progression that leads us to a fruitful life in Christ. Observe the way that this passage instructs to "add to". Take note also that we begin with a "whereby", indicating that by that which was outlined in the previous verses we now have the following. By the divine power through Jesus Christ we have "exceeding great and precious promises"

"Whereby are given unto us exceeding great and precious promises: that by these ye might be partakers of the divine nature, having escaped the corruption that is in the world through lust And beside this, giving all diligence, add to your faith virtue; and to virtue knowledge; And to knowledge temperance; and to temperance patience; and to patience godliness; And to godliness brotherly kindness; and to brotherly kindness charity. For if these things be in you, and abound, they make you that ye shall neither be barren nor unfruitful in the knowledge of our Lord Jesus Christ. But he that lacketh these things is blind, and cannot see afar off, and hath forgotten that he was purged from his old sins."

The pinnacle is "charity" or love. We are to build upon a foundation that is first given to us in Christ Jesus our Lord, and add to our faith in Him virtue, then knowledge, then temperance, next comes patience, bringing godliness…then it hits the bump in the road that we seem to struggle with…brotherly kindness.

Verse 8 declares that "if these things be in you", if all of these attributes are building blocks in your life then and only then will you be fruitful and bare knowledge of Christ. If we do not have these, then we are short sighted and eventually it becomes a hindrance to being purged of sin.

We usually focus on how much faith we have. Talking at length about how virtuous and knowledgeable we are. In most cases we can subdue the old man long enough to make people believe that we are quite temperate and patient…and oh how kind…when we want to turn it on. All of this making us appear to be quite full of Godliness.

I would ask, at this point, why wouldn't Godliness be the pinnacle and all of this love stuff be listed prior to the Godliness? Perhaps there is a subtle message that Peter is giving. (I'm sure Peter had known many who appeared to be Godly, yet, couldn't go through the purification process to a higher plane in God.) Many never attain brotherly kindness and ultimately charity.

Sadly, so many loose out at this point. The race becomes too hot and weariness takes its toll on the spirits of men and we succumb to the fatigue of life's bombardment and find the easier path of turning our heads. Pretending not see the need of our brother or sister. Just as an ostrich would stick its head in the sand, we too think that as long as I do not see it, it will go away. Only to be devoured by the enemy of love.

In our lacking it is no wonder that we find, as **2 Peter 1:8** explains, that we *"are barren and unfruitful"*.

When love does not grow to the will of our Heavenly Father, the flow of blessing will cause a Dead Sea affect where our bowls of compassion have plugged up our witness.

I've found that the closer you get to the Lord, in reading His Word and Prayer, there is a tendency to desire to separate yourself more to the purpose of spending time with God. Just as Moses went to the mountain and stayed for forty days, we too begin to feel the thrill of remaining in the presence of God. It can be both fulfilling and self exalting.

If the fulfillment of remaining in God's presence isn't balanced with caring and loving others, we will eventually dry up spiritually.

This relationship with God is designed to flow into us, and then out of us into others. Causing a chain reaction where our connection with God will inspire love and good works in others to also draw closer to God…not just to us.

Although the Children of Israel were at fault in their panic of building a golden calf to worship, because Moses was withdrawn to the mountain with God for such a lengthy time. We also cannot be too critical of the sense of loss that they must have felt. It does point out some of the same tendencies that we see in churches today.

The "cats" away, the mice will play.

While our experiences may elevate one versus another into higher callings or services, the Love of God constrains and levels the field to make us equals.

Burnt Dinner + Love = Happiness

Remember the honeymoon? No! Not just those first few days or weeks when you were off to Cancun or the Bahamas. Back when it didn't matter if the clothes were washed on time, or if the meal was just right, or if he was slim, fat, tall, short, hair was feathered back or straight....as long as you had love, everything was a "bed of roses"!

> **Proverbs 15:17**, *"Better is a dinner of herbs where love is, than a stalled ox and hatred therewith."*

Solomon says that a bowl of lettuce with love was better than having all the promise of a juicy steak and living with strife!

The stalled ox was symbolic of a majestic thing of promise. A fat calf in your stall was a great sign of prosperity!

Love Is...a Tattoo?!

The wisest man on earth said...

> **Songs of Solomon 8:6**, *"Set me as a seal upon thine heart, as a seal upon thine arm: for love is strong as death; jealousy is cruel as the grave: the coals thereof are coals of fire, which hath a most vehement flame."*

Notice the twinkle in Solomon's eye as he describes love as a "tattoo on the arm". The word picture is quite vivid!

Love and jealousy are almost relatives in this passage. Both have a bond as sure as death and the grave that follows. When love is interjected, it is as sure as the fact that one will eventually see death...love never faileth! But, the flip side of death is how empty a grave can be. Jealousy brings that emptiness to friendships and relationships.

Though love is as sure, to bind two souls together, as death, so is jealousy the killer that will destroy love between us. When you find jealousy you have found an empty grave site.

If we are honest, we will admit that there are way too many grave sites along the path of our past...love that was destroyed by jealousy.

> **Romans 13:10**, *"Love worketh no ill to his neighbour: therefore love is the fulfilling of the law."*

If we could only love, in its purest sense, as God loves, there would be no issues with all the sins that so many constantly battle. Adultery, murder, stealing, bearing false witness would all be a thing of the past. Love does conquer all!

It is the fulfillment of the law. The law makes a futile effort of injecting love. But what the law cannot do, the love of God will do!

Have you noticed when an individual repents, has their sinful past washed away through waters of baptism in the name Jesus, and are filled with the Holy Spirit that things, that they struggled with their whole life, begin to fall off? It is such an amazing phenomena to see the love of God at work in a person's life. Many things do not need to be taught…the life just changes from lawless to lawful. That is truly the fulfillment of the law by allowing love to flourish.

The Condition of Love

As we close out this chapter on love, we would miss the whole point if we did not look at *1 John 4:7-21*.

John admonishes, "let us love one another". "Let" is a conscience decision to actively love. You first must let it happen in your life. Pride and many other enemies of love will keep us from loving, so we must work to "let" it grow in us.

Our Heavenly Father was the initiator of love. While we were yet in sin he loved us. Verse 11 points to the fact that if God so loved us…(so, being the extent in which he pursued us)…then we "ought also…(in like manner)…to love one another.

To what extent would you go to love someone back to God? It is important you know. These verses give a glimpse at how our ability to even confess Jesus as the Son of God all hinges on whether we love our brother. If we can't love our brother, whom we have seen, how then can we love God, who we have not seen?

The final barometer for whether we truly love God or not is how we love humanity.

God is love. One of the many attributes of God is love in its purest sense of the word. He cannot separate himself from loving humanity. And, to be in Christ Jesus, God manifested to us in flesh, we too must love humanity.

If all the law, the prophets, the purpose of the Messiah, and redemption its self all hinge on loving humanity, then I for one must confess that I need more of God in my life. Without his love working in me, I can never love people as He loves them.

If love is that important, what shall we do with it? Love your neighbor as yourself.

Love without boundaries or limitations, love them like Jesus...

> **Love Them Like Jesus lyrics**
> **Songwriters:** *Hall, Mark; Herms, Bernie;*
>
> *The love of her life is drifting away*
> *They're losing the fight for another day*
> *The life that she's known is falling apart*
> *A fatherless home, a child's broken heart*
>
> *You're holding her hand, you're straining for words*
> *You trying to make sense of it all*
> *She's desperate for hope, darkness clouding her view*
> *She's looking to you*
>
> *Just love her like Jesus, carry her to Him*
> *His yoke is easy, His burden is light*
> *You don't need the answers to all of life's questions*
> *Just know that He loves her and stay by her side*
> *And love her like Jesus, love her like Jesus*
>
> *The gifts lie in wait, in a room painted blue*
> *Little blessing from Heaven would be there soon*
> *Hope fades in the night, blue skies turn to gray*
> *As the little one slips away*

You're holding their hand, you're straining for words
You're trying to make sense of it all
They're desperate for hope, darkness clouding their view
And they're looking to you

Just love them like Jesus, carry them to Him
His yoke is easy, His burden is light
You don't need the answers to all of life's questions
Just know that He loves them and stay by their side
And love them like Jesus

Lord of all creation holds our lives in His hands
The God of all the nations holds our lives in His hands
The Rock of our salvation holds our lives in His hands
He cares for them just as He cares for you

So love them like Jesus, love them like Jesus
You don't need the answers to all of life's questions
Just know that He loves them and stay by their side
And love them like Jesus, love them like Jesus
Love them like Jesus, love them like Jesus

"It is not how much you do, but how much love you put into the doing that matters." ~ Mother Teresa

CARE BY GOING TO THEIR AID

CHAPTER 7

"People only bring up your past when they are intimidated by your present." ~ **Wise Man Si**

My dad was the victim of a tragic accident several years ago, which left him a quadriplegic. This condition required him to have an aid come to his home each day for several hours in the morning and a couple hours in the evening. The aid had many responsibilities, too numerous to name them all in detail. Suffice to say that their sole purpose was to insure my dad was cleaned up, watch for symptoms of infections or disease, get him dressed, and into his "wheel barrel" (his affectionate name for his electric wheelchair) so that he can spend a few hours each day with some similitude of independence or freedom to move about.

When the aid does not show, his whole world goes into chaos.

When you rely on an aid to this degree it is virtually impossible to describe the emotions that one goes through when they cannot get out of bed. The importance of the aid's consistency is unspeakable. It cannot be put into words the need for someone that really cares and doesn't take the afflicted individuals' well being lightly.

It doesn't take more than an hour or so to know how much an aid cares. They may be compensated the very same monetarily, but they shouldn't be. The aid that cares will be prompt on arrival, be understanding when the patient is in an emotional upheaval, and will do anything that will make that individual comfortable. The only thing that would hold them back is when it is not moral or not in the best interest of the individual, even though they think it would be. If the handicapped person makes a total mess of their bed or wheel chair, they clean it up without scolding or reprimand. Aides will take into consideration the handicap and not require them to be as someone that is whole.

It is our calling to go to the aid of those that have fallen. Yes, it's a messy job that requires some humility and spirit of a servant, but its still our calling to care.

Response to "Backsliding"

When someone backslides, falters, falls off the wagon...our reaction should never be to attempt to instruct or fix them. There will be a time and place for instruction, but, in most cases, they already know the answer...they just need to know we care. So, make sure they know you love them by going the extra mile to pray, smile, and encourage them. Even if asked, don't fall in the trap of advising until there is a change of direction and heart. And, even then, proceed with caution!

Those that are married can attest to the fact that there are times where it is better to be silent! Should I rephrase as, sincerely silent. Meaning, listen but don't try to fix the problem. My wife has started some very innocent conversations by asking my thoughts, but, as she begins to lay out the scenario my radar begins to go off and I try my best not to blurt out advice. To the best of my ability I attempt to refrain from going into the fix-it mode and simply listen to her day. At the end, or even during the giving of details, I may say something like, "Wow, that's bad." or "I hear ya." , but, it isn't a good time to provide advise on how to solve the problem. Otherwise, I have found that it is a trap where all the issues of the day become focused on YOU!

In like manner, when someone is sliding down a slippery slope it isn't time to throw them a backpack full of provisions for the journey. All that would be is like a bundle of rocks that only quickens the descent down the slope. Its time to toss them "a rope of hope, not a pack of reasoning". They may reject the rope altogether, but doing nothing will only deepen their feelings of despair. The rope is a lifeline of kindness that they will need to take the initiative to grab hold of and begin the journey back up the slope. Your ability to show kindness, even if they are cussing you as they slide, will be the only hope of restoring them and perhaps it will be their salvation.

The real question is, do you care enough...or do you care at all?

Who Lifted Who?

When we come to the realization that if it were not for the Lord, I could never make heaven my home, only then will we reach to the hurting and broken as God desires. Let this song be a reminder of who lifted us from the pit we where in.

Love Lifted Me:
I was sinking deep in sin, far from the peaceful shore,
Very deeply stained within, sinking to rise no more,
But the Master of the sea, heard my despairing cry,
From the waters lifted me, now safe am I.
Refrain

Love lifted me! Love lifted me!
When nothing else could help
Love lifted me!

All my heart to Him I give, ever to Him I'll cling
In His blessèd presence live, ever His praises sing,
Love so mighty and so true, merits my soul's best songs,
Faithful, loving service too, to Him belongs.

Souls in danger look above, Jesus completely saves,
He will lift you by His love, out of the angry waves.
He's the Master of the sea, billows His will obey,
He your Savior wants to be, be saved today.

If we can let the same love that picked us up flow through us to others we will change the lives, and perhaps the final destination, of people.

We are all judgmental. By picking and choosing who we will help or not, we've placed ourselves in the judgment seat. Because we have placed limitations on who and what we will reach to, then the bowels of compassion have been stopped up. This condition has brought barrenness to the womb of the church.

Reach as you would want Jesus to reach to you. Don't let the issue be that you feel worthy, for that is pride and God cannot dwell in a house with pride.

U.S. Soldier's Creed

The Army creed has the phrase "*I will never leave a fallen comrade.*" which Christians would do well to take notes and apply the principles when looking at caring for others.

May we be reminded of **Ephesians 6:12,** *"For we wrestle not against flesh and blood, but against principalities, against powers, against the rulers of the darkness of this world, against spiritual wickedness in high places."*

The battle is not for physical properties, but for a spiritual territory. We are not fighting for us and against them, in a physical realm, but it is against the wickedness of one who is the opposition to Jehovah God Himself!

Reach for the fallen comrade in every circumstance. There is a crown waiting for those that do.

Fight For Your Brother

> *Nehemiah 4:14,* *"And I looked, and rose up, and said unto the nobles, and to the rulers, and to the rest of the people, Be not ye afraid of them: remember the Lord, which is great and terrible, and fight for your brethren, your sons, and your daughters, your wives, and your houses."*

Nehemiah stood in the face of adversity and declared to the people to stand and not be afraid! I am interested in how he motivates the people.

Notice the motivation that Nehemiah used.

First, your brethren. "I got your back!" attitude! A spirit of camaraderie that we are in this together and if I let up I may loose you to the enemy, so, I fight for you!

Secondly, your family. For those you care for and love. Though a warrior, I am also tender enough to care for those in who trust me to protect them. I've heard the meekest of men say, "Mess with anything I have but don't come into my home! I will take action to stop you!" That motivation is a feeling of responsibility to those who look to you for protection.

Thirdly, your house. The fight wasn't just for the lumber, brick, mortar, and shingles. It was a statement of place. They have just returned to a place promised to their forefathers and it was a fight for holding onto promises of God.

All of these motivations caused the people to set their jaw and prepare to be aggressive. Let the enemy come, they were determined to protect what God had promised.

Catch the wisdom of Nehemiah! If he would have started with "save your house", then men would have grabbed their individual promises and crawled off into a corner waiting for someone to try and take what was rightfully theirs. If he would have only said, "save your sons, daughters, and wives" then this too would have given an out for them to retreat and surround their individual families and fight off any that tried to harm them.

In either of these cases it falls directly to the first article of war, "divide and conquer". If each man would have retreated to protect his own, the division would have allowed the enemy to come in and pick them off one or two at a time. But, Nehemiah started with, "fight for your brethren"! Fight for your fellow countryman. Don't back down because you are standing for a higher purpose than just your own possessions. Your brother is your comrade and comrades don't leave you standing without protecting your back.

When you are vulnerable, hurt, being crushed by the enemy, at a point of despair, your brethren are there to fight. Not just for themselves, but for you. Your brethren are going to Fight in your behalf! Because if my brother falls, then it will also make me vulnerable…so, I fight for my brother!

It is not a passive "I love you brother", when it is convenient or when others can hear. It is a warrior's cry of motivation… "FIGHT FOR YOUR BRETHREN!" I mean, fight FOR them. Be aggressive! Not against them, but for them. Fight off the enemy. Be determined not to keep them down. Don't quit until they have been protected from the enemy! Have their back! Destroy, crush, and annihilate the enemy of their souls! For, if you do not, you will be the next focus of the enemy's attention.

This is love…it is the ability to see the circumstances, weaknesses, and even failures and still go to bat for your brethren. Its not about friendship alone…it is the love of God that will take us to a cross and still be concerned about a thief.

Don't Defraud God

I Thessalonians 4:6-9 proclaims that we shouldn't need to be taught further about loving our brothers and sisters because it is a basic principle from God Himself.

> *"That no man go beyond and defraud his brother in any matter: because that the Lord is the avenger of all such, as we also have forewarned you and testified. For God hath not called us unto uncleanness, but unto holiness. He therefore that despiseth, despiseth not man, but God, who hath also given unto us his holy Spirit. But as touching brotherly love ye need not that I write unto you: for ye yourselves are taught of God to love one another."*

Defraud is defined as *"to over reach: - get an advantage, defraud, make a gain"*.

Our brother is not a stepping stone to be used for our own gain.

When one would use another to get advantage, his offense is not with humanity but is with the Creator. How serious is that?!

It is a worldly view of humanity to think of them as pawns in a game. Expendable commodities, to save the greater whole. To throw them under the bus is an atrocity against Yahweh! To gain advantage by manipulation, stroking, making alliances for the express purpose of gain is a sin against God Himself.

I recall pretending to be a pet dog (how low can you go?) by barking and acting like a foolish mutt, to get my sisters to give me their french fries. Missy wouldn't fall for the ploy, but, Mendy in her usual loving way would feed "the dog" and enjoy every minute of it. Not realizing that I had just used her for my gain! Yes, confession is good for the soul!! Although it was a child's game, it shows how foolish people will act to patronize those around them to get some kind of advantage to make gain.

God does not honor such fake acts of love. If a thought comes to mind, which brings a sense of conviction about ways you are

using others, repent and STOP! God already knows our plots.
Worse yet, when it finally dawns on the person we have used, it
could destroy them for ever. Their faith in men and God would
be destroyed and potentially lost forever. Who could sleep at
night knowing this could be the potential outcome?

Thinking Like A Goat!

With a cold weather front coming in, I thought I would put the
goats (8 in all) in the barn, for their own comfort. So, I took the
feeders inside, dropped some feed in and called the goats. They
came running in and began to fight over every little grain. By
the time they had finished eating, I had the barn closed off so
that they couldn't go out in the cold nasty rain. As their attention
turned from the feed they began to look at one another. All of a
sudden, a couple of the bigger goats began to run across the pen
and head butt each other, slamming them into the walls. I
thought, for the safety of the smaller yearlings, I would separate
them into another pen inside the barn. I was successful in
getting three of the four smaller goats separated easily, but the
one that was left (her name is "tiny") was being chased all
around the pen and being slammed against the walls repeatedly
by the bigger goats...because they could! I finally cohersed Tiny
into the "small goat" pen and felt some satisfaction in knowing
that she wouldn't get hurt by the big goats picking on her. About
that time I heard a "thud" coming from the small goat pen! I
went to investigate, and found Tiny running across the pen and
slamming another yearling nanny, that was bigger than her, into
the walls! Repeatedly, she kept chasing the other goat around
and head butting her! Then, while the offended goat ran from
Tiny, another usually very mellow nanny, turned around and
added an extra slam!!

As I watched this unfold, my heart began to sink with heaviness.
How typical! Not just of goats, but people have the same
tendencies about them! You put them with one group and they
may get slammed against the wall, but, you show them a little
kindness and move them to another group and they rise up and
begin to slam others. I will never cease to be amazed at how
natural it is for us to be critical of others, and how easily one can
fall into the "herd" nature where we have to find the "pecking
order". And once an individual has slipped in the slightest, we
"dog pile" to insure they are not just down but they stay down!

My mind began to reflect on some of my own experiences over the last few years and it didn't take long to feel a compassion for the goat that was being repeatedly slammed into the walls...I began to ask the goats (out loud), "Why? Why are you doing this to one another??" Of course they would stop for a moment and just look at me with their heads a little tilted. Who knows what they were thinking. Probably, "hmmmm, why isn't he joining in on the fun?!"

There will be several groups of people that may read this...some will relate to being slammed around...some will look at this with their heads tilted asking why others aren't joining in on the fun and games...then, there will be others who will simply keep eating hay while ignoring the hurt that others feel.

Next time you think about using your power, position, or just your own lack of self-esteem to motivate a slam to someone else, think about a goat and how silly they look...

Precious Commodities Are Lost

> **Proverbs 17:14**, "*The beginning of strife is as when one letteth out water: therefore leave off contention, before it be meddled with.*"

Just a handful of words packed full of wisdom.

Imagine with me that we are in a desert place and our survival is predicated upon all in the group, and the most important commodity that we posses is a couple canteens of precious drops of water left in them. Food has its importance, but none can live long without water.

Lack of water will cause internal organs to shut down. Simultaneously the brain begins to become delirious, causing blurred vision and lack of control. Strength is sapped from the muscles and one will lay down to sleep and never awaken. Water is the life line to making the journey.

Its tough enough trying to keep the enemy from finding a way to shoot a hole in the canteens, but how foolish would it be for one, in the group, to take a lid off the canteens and pour out the final drops of water. Or, for one to walk over and deliberately shoot holes in the bottom of the canteen. It would be suicide!

Strife and contention causes spiritual suicide!

Solomon challenges to "leave off contentions, before it be meddled with". In other words, avoid strife and contention at all cost! It will be like taking the canteen and pouring the water into the sand. Like throwing a lifeline overboard and deliberately letting the secured end unravel and fall into the raging sea as well. As crazy as sewing your mouth and nostrils shut and think you will still be able to breath.

Communication and humility will be the cork that plugs the holes that contention has caused in a relationship. Self absorbed agendas, un-flexibility, and lack of time will make room for doubts, leading to suspicion, and shortly followed by strife and contention that drains the life blood out of any relationship.

Be quick to go to your brother. Be willing to receive a brother. Be willing to forgive and build upon the strengths and not focus on the weaknesses.

Can You Intercede?

When you have no other reason to care, yet you intercede for their need, there is power, in that, it shatters all reason and selfishness!

Intercessory Prayer Will Move Mountains! But, do we care enough to become humbled in prayer for our brother?

Sure we do, for those that we agree with or that fall into our cliché. But do we have enough of God in us to pray for those in whom we dislike or mistrust?

It would do us well to have an old fashion confession. Instead of pretending that we have it all together, in fear of loosing "our" following, we hide behind reputations. And, oh how we protect our reputations! I know that a good name is better to be had than many riches, but, God loves a humble and contrite heart. Not a hidden agenda heart that only shows its self behind closed doors or on a phone where no one else can know except the one that has just received the stab of a "good ol fashion tongue lash'n".

60

The Apostle James had some closing thoughts that would be good advise as we close out this chapter. The admonishments bring to focus who and what we really are.

> **James 5:16**, *"Confess your faults one to another, and pray one for another, that ye may be healed. The effectual fervent prayer of a righteous man availeth much."*

The higher we get…the bigger the reputation…the more pious we become, the harder it is to confess. Yet, it is directly linked to our prayers being answered and even personal healing.

I wonder if James doesn't attempt to show the contrast between one who cannot confess and that of a righteous man. The righteous will confess their faults…readily…and in thus doing, their prayers avail much in the sight of God. Lack of confession makes one's prayers of nun-affect.

> **James 5:19**, *"Brethren, if any of you do err from the truth, and one convert him; Let him know, that he which converteth the sinner from the error of his way shall save a soul from death, and shall hide a multitude of sins."*

Convert can also be interpreted as revert. When a brother has stumbled, your goal is to revert him back to his previous ways. Sure, he is a sinner! But the conversion is done by hiding a multitude of sins. We must get more acquainted with the "reverting" process and less with the condemning attitude.

Are you willing to intercede? Christians tend to do well with it until it costs them time or energy. Push beyond yourself

As we embark on a very important part of "Cultivating a Culture of Caring" I am compelled to be very plain from the outset. There is no human alive that has not used words to harm others. No exemptions! No free passes!!

I have to say this because the individual that says, this chapter isn't for me, is the first group I want to speak to. Why? Because, if we do not realize our human nature, then we will never be controlled by the Spirit of God. Let 1 Corinthians, 13:1 be a perpetual reminder, *"Though I speak with the tongues of men and of angels, and have not charity, I am become as sounding brass, or a tinkling cymbal."*

All that we say must be filtered through charity. If love conquers all, then, let it conquer our tongue. Let it provide speech therapy that makes our conversations acceptable in the eyes of God.

The person that complains about everyone else is, in many cases, the root of the problem. Complaints do not have their foundation in truth or faith.

It's no wonder that the Holy Spirit infilling is evidenced by speaking in other tongues. A complete submission to the Spirit and allowing it to take the unruly tongue and causing it to speak words that do not come from the brain waves of learning. Many are intimidated with that acclaim. If I may explain further, the speaking in tongues is not a physical act of God grabbing hold of the tongue and making it flap around to create "jibber jabber".

In my experience it is a submission of my mind to the Holy Spirit and it speaks through my tongue in a language I have not learned. It is a Divine inspiration that is carried by waves of the Spirit as it takes up residence in one's heart. From that point, though, we must submit daily to the Spirit's leading. Otherwise we will only have this experience as a trophy on the mantle to brag about. It must be dusted off daily and let it lead our every thought, and ultimately the words that we speak. For, in them, life and death are generated.

Words

Words can be a powerful tool. They have the potential to kill or make alive, crush or caress, lift or lash. They can build up or tear down, strengthen or weaken; they are powerful to cause unity or division, brotherly love or dissention, self-esteem or lack of self worth. It has been said that even a plant will grow with soothing words spoken to it.

It is imperative to surround yourself, especially in times of discouragement, with people who will speak truth, love, and strength into your life. Many times the "truth" spoken in "love" will be your "strength" as well. We cannot sidestep the need for honesty, as long as there is a track record of trust with the individual that speaks honestly about change.

> ***Proverbs 25:11-13,*** *"A word fitly spoken is like apples of gold in pictures of silver. As an earring of gold, and an ornament of fine gold, so is a wise reprover upon an obedient ear. As the cold of snow in the time of harvest, so is a faithful messenger to them that send him: for he refresheth the soul of his masters."*

There is nothing more valuable, and even more adorning, than the one who brings a timely word of instruction to one that is willing to hear.

"As the cold of snow in the time of harvest…refresheth the soul" This is not speaking of a storm with sleeting rain, hail, and a foot of white snow to smother the harvest. It speaks of the fall months when the workers are feverishly striving to get the harvest finished, in a place where temperatures typically are hot and miserable, the snow will begin to fall high up in the mountains. Bringing a cool breeze to aid the efforts and boost the energy levels, and the streams flow with abundance of fresh cool water melting from high above. This refreshing brings less stress to the servants, the harvest is not hindered, bringing a relief to the master of the harvest.

So it is with words spoken in an hour of hot adversity in one's life. When it seems that the whole world is crashing down with weights and pressures of life pushing from every side. The cool breeze of an encouraging word and a dip of cool water from the stream of wisdom will satisfy one's mind and heart.

Ten Ways To Be A Friend

1. Listen - without interrupting
2. Speak - without accusing
3. Give - without sparing
4. Pray - without ceasing
5. Answer - without arguing
6. Share - without pretending
7. Enjoy - without complaint
8. Trust - without wavering
9. Forgive - without punishing
10. Promise - without forgetting

Most of us have experienced the power of what people say.
Good and bad!

> **Proverbs 18:21**, *"Words kill, words give life; they're either poison or fruit you choose."*

Where Do We Find Meaning In Life?

In his book *"Man's Search for Meaning"*, Victor Frankl makes the statement *"Ever more people today have the means to live, but no meaning to live for"*. What a profound observation!

Victor was a survivor of the concentration camps during the Second World War, and became a neurologist and psychiatrist. His observations of those who survived longest in concentration camps were not necessarily the strongest or those with the greatest will to live. But, it was those who retained a sense of control over their environment. It was those who would go from compound to compound comforting others and giving their last morsel of bread to others that seemed to have the most grip on hope of a brighter tomorrow. The giving out to others was a distinct sign that they knew the circumstances but believed that if they could help motivate people to hold on one more day, they would be able to walk out together. Using his experiences he traced the motivation to continue to live. He believed that it was neither pleasure nor power but meaning that motivated.
With the divorce rate around fifty percent, it is increasingly probable that you will have a loved one tell you they wish to get

out. Then, you add onto that, the probability of a child walking away without cause, a loved one suddenly taken from this life unexpectedly, a job playing out without any grounds for dismissal, or perhaps it could be a fire that destroys a home and all that you own, an accident that leaves you with doctor bills and health issues that seem to continue to spiral into further debt and despair. It is important for us to realize that we need others to survive the rigors of life and all that it can throw at us. Few will breeze through an entire lifetime without going through a time of disparaging circumstances.

Life happens! And when it does, we must be built on a solid rock of faith and surrounded by a line of friendships that are willing to take a risk for you.

Deeper the Depths, Deeper the Cuts

If you are one that has stepped out in faith and went deeper, only to be hurt more deeply than others, remember that the ladder is shakiest at the top.

Have you ever felt this way?

> *Psalms 107:23-27, "They that go down to the sea in ships, that do business in great waters; These see the works of the LORD, and his wonders in the deep. For he commandeth, and raiseth the stormy wind, which lifteth up the waves thereof. They mount up to the heaven, they go down again to the depths: their soul is melted because of trouble. They reel to and fro, and stagger like a drunken man, and are at their wits' end."*

Those that are willing to "do business in great waters" are more likely to "see the works of the Lord". God's wonders are found in the deep, but the risk is also greater. You are no longer in the wading pool splashing around giggling with the children, you now find yourself with waves that reach into the heavens, and valleys that plummet into the depths, trouble increases, and you are shoved from one side of trouble to the other until you are oblivious to where you are at, and find yourself at your wits' end.

Many want the rewards of going into the uncharted territory of the Spirit but only the hungry will risk everything to go into the depths.

Here is the promise to those that will take the journey…

> **Psalms 107:28-30**, *"Then they cry unto the LORD in their trouble, and he bringeth them out of their distresses. He maketh the storm a calm, so that the waves thereof are still. Then are they glad because they be quiet; so he bringeth them unto their desired haven."*

When you have jumped out of the boat to walk on water, and soon begin to sink, as Peter did, it is time to cry unto the Lord! The promise is that God will hear and bring you out!

I know it seems that some things are self inflicted. You took a chance and after getting into the deep, you find the tumultuous situation greater than you had expected. You stuck your neck out and someone chopped it off!! Well, Jesus knows all about your trouble…be comforted with that.

After a testing, God will make the waves to be still and lift us to a haven to rest in quiet. Be at peace with that understanding. It isn't failure when we step out in faith and find ourselves weaker than the challenges…Jesus cares!!

If you've been hurt, it is a natural feeling to feel that no one cares. There may be a thousand people who really do care, but, when you are left to your own thoughts, and no one calls with words of encouragement, know two things will cure our disparing soul…

First, the Word of God accompanied with prayer will set the sail in the right direction, and give peace when the storm is raging!

Secondly, your motivation must be to look to others and help them. Give them your last piece of bread and see if it doesn't return to your pressed down, shaken together, and running over with God's grace and strength.

"Who Cares?" Jesus does…and others will once the trial has passed and strength will return. Hold to Gods unchanging hand!

CHAPTER 9

"NFL players in New Orleans aren't the only people who claim to be "Saints", while trying to injure those around them."

Understanding the value of an Individual

It is amazing how that theatrics will so vividly portray the personality of each character. The viewer is moved by each, and even emotionally connected by the various personalities. Every part is intricate to the whole. To fully see the plot, you cannot single out one actor and let them read their lines alone. The continuity of many voices, like a choir, will allow the onlooker to visualize the scenes as they come together to tell a story. Only then will it move the crowd to laughter or tears, based on how the playwright's theme unfolds.

In similar fashion we must value each member. The lack of appreciation for each individual and what they bring to the body, will cause a lacking to the ability of the whole to accomplish their goals. In devaluing, lowering the value, of each "member" you always cut off potentials that would feed into the body. It doesn't matter if it is the toe or the ear, each have a function that goes beyond the personal preferences that we so many times cater too.

Paul makes reference to how the many varying entities are molded into one, "in Christ", to the point that the members are one "of" another.

> **Romans 12:5** *"So we, being many, are one body in Christ, and every one members one of another."*

It is not one to another. Nor are we one only in Christ, but, just as the analogies for marriage, the two pieces of paper are glued together and when you try to separate them you damage both. We are so fitly joined together, in Christ Jesus, that our separation tears a part of our individuality away. As a woven fabric, we cannot have a single thread pulled out that will not affect the stability of the balance of the fabric. The church, so too often, has become an "irregular" product that is viewed by

the world as second rate.
It is no wonder they consider the church another country club to join if it is financially or socially beneficial.

Understanding the individuality that is required to make the whole to become self sustaining is crucial. Notice in the following Scripture that it makes reference to "also is Christ"…

> ***1 Corinthians 12:12-14***, "*For as the body is one, and hath many members, and all the members of that one body, being many, are one body: **so also is Christ**. For by one Spirit are we all baptized into one body, whether we be Jews or Gentiles, whether we be bond or free; and have been all made to drink into one Spirit. For the body is not one member, but many.*"

All said and done, the completion of the body is a reflection of the Head, which is Christ. The dysfunction of the members is a reflection of the connection with the Head and it's every intention. We know that the Head (Christ) is in good working condition, but, the paralysis of the body shows a disconnect between the Head and the various members.

God is not looking for a "cookie cutter" body…He desires to use a vast array of personalities. As many as there are individuals, so are the parts that are needed.

> ***1 Corinthians 12:18-19***, "*But now hath God set the members every one of them in the body, as it hath pleased him. And if they were all one member, where were the body*"

From the leadership to every member, all struggle with a desire for every member to be the same. Think the same, respond the same, look the same, and live the same. And, the same is like "ME"! Or you!

Because we see what we do, then it is natural to think all should be like me.

Don't misunderstand my message. I'm not speaking of finding boundaries and teaching guidelines and even restraint when and where it is needed. What I am saying is that each person is an individual and how they process information can become an asset to the body if leadership has wisdom to utilize the differences.

The phrase, "as it hath pleased Him", is a key statement to recon with. God adds to the body and plugs them in so that it can function more completely, for the purpose of winning the lost.

Paul's statement, "where were the body", holds a bit of humor in it. If everyone was an eye, it would be an interesting body with thousands and millions of eyes. Where would be the functions that are needed to sustain the millions of eyes? The goal is to become complete in God, by adding the parts and pieces to the body.

Each part must willingly trust all the others. If a organ is rejected, it becomes unable to function with the rest of the body. A valuable part is lost.

You will not achieve this goal of utopia…a normal functioning mass…without gathering all the parts.
Ezekiel could speak to the yard of bones but until they came together and began to grow sinew, muscle, veins, nerves, organs, and skin…the prophetic would have never came to pass.

Caring for the body will be achieved by having appreciation for the differences that each individual brings to the whole. And the head is glorified!

> **1Peter 5:7,** *"Casting all your care upon him; for he careth for you."*

Chemistry

When speaking of sports or a team of people attempting to accomplish a goal. The term "chemistry" will come up regularly. It's a term that identifies one of the basic qualities needed to succeed when you have more than one person on a job. It speaks to the ability to mix all the ingredients and still have an affective whole.

There are some chemicals that you do not mix.

My son and I worked on an experiment once where you take a bottle of Coke and you drop 2-3 Mentos in and quickly screw the lid down. The Mentos will have a carbon dioxide reaction to the acids in the drink and the fizz will build until it finally explodes. The burst of soda can go as high as 10-18 feet in the air. Ours didn't do as well as we would have liked, but, it did shoot up in the air further than I could have imagined.

Some people are proud to be the "mentos". Every time they are injected into an environment, it isn't long before they have caused a fizz and it explodes!

Without the working of the Holy Spirit in our lives, we all have this potential, when the natural chemicals are not compatible. But with the power of the Holy Ghost we can be transformed to become what God would have us to be.

It takes all the Fruits of the Spirit at times, but it can be done if we seek God for guidance, and we follow after Him to accomplish the purpose.

Jehovah Seeks To Love Humanity Over All

Isaiah chapter 1 provides a glimpse into the heart of God. Although he has established the rites and rituals to remind us of him, yet, he would trade it all for us to love humanity.

Isaiah 1:11-18...

> 11) *To what purpose is the multitude of your sacrifices unto me? saith the LORD: I am full of the burnt offerings of rams, and the fat of fed beasts; and I delight not in the blood of bullocks, or of lambs, or of he goats.*
> 12) *When ye come to appear before me, who hath required this at your hand, to tread my courts?*
> 13) *Bring no more vain oblations; incense is an abomination unto me; the new moons and sabbaths, the calling of assemblies, I cannot away with; it is iniquity, even the solemn meeting.*
> 14) *Your new moons and your appointed feasts my soul hateth: they are a trouble unto me; I am weary to bear them.*

15) And when ye spread forth your hands, I will hide mine eyes from you: yea, when ye make many prayers, I will not hear: your hands are full of blood.

16) Wash you, make you clean; put away the evil of your doings from before mine eyes; cease to do evil;

17) Learn to do well; seek judgment, relieve the oppressed, judge the fatherless, plead for the widow.

18) Come now, and let us reason together, saith the LORD: though your sins be as scarlet, they shall be as white as snow; though they be red like crimson, they shall be as wool.

I repeat, God established these rituals, sacrifices, incense, and feasts! Yet He is sick of them! In verse 16 and 17 he lists some things that he desires…let's take a look.

- *Wash you, make you clean* – isn't that the signature act that God requires of mankind? To be in His presence, we must wash first.
- *Put away* – He mentions two areas of evil actions, first what you see and then to cease what you do. Our greatest temptations begin with what we see. If the sight of temptation causes us to act, then it require a ceasing of our evil actions.
- *Learn to do well!* – You mean it doesn't come natural? Not a chance!! Learn here means to practice until you are doing the opposite of evil.
- *Seek judgment* – Notice that this is tied directly into the "learn to do well". Its an extension or definition of the learning. Seek to have correct judgment. Or, could we say, righteousness.
- *Relieve the oppressed* – The word Relieve is interpreted "make straight". Smooth out the road and make the way easier for the oppressed. Stick up for those under oppression. Be one who stands up to the bully and helps the humble.
- *Judge the fatherless* – Vindicate the fatherless. Don't take advantage of them. Be the covering that they lack by not having their biological parents.
- *Plead for the widow* – Contend for her. Go to her aid in her defenseless state.

You want your prayers to be hindered? Then do the opposite of the above. If you want God's blessings, then not only do these things, but be fervent about doing them.

God is interested in how we deal with the weakest among us.

Caution To Focus On The Lowly

Isaiah goes on to call Israel out further…

Isaiah 1:22-28,

> 22) *Thy silver is become dross, thy wine mixed with water:*
> 23) *Thy princes are rebellious, and companions of thieves: every one loveth gifts, and followeth after rewards: they judge not the fatherless, neither doth the cause of the widow come unto them.*
> 24) *Therefore saith the Lord, the LORD of hosts, the mighty One of Israel, Ah, I will ease me of mine adversaries, and avenge me of mine enemies:*
> 25) *And I will turn my hand upon thee, and purely purge away thy dross, and take away*
> 26) *all thy tin:*
> 27) *And I will restore thy judges as at the first, and thy counsellors as at the beginning: afterward thou shalt be called, The city of righteousness, the faithful city.*
> 28) *Zion shall be redeemed with judgment, and her converts with righteousness.*
> 29) *And the destruction of the transgressors and of the sinners shall be together, and they that forsake the LORD shall be consumed.*

These warnings continually flow throughout Scripture, and they seem to be wholly directed to those in leadership and those sitting in judgment, or, those who could make a difference, yet they consciously decide to turn their head away from the lowly. Those who need protection, safe keeping, compassion, and help are forsaken while the rich get richer.

- *Silver becomes dross* – With this lack of concern, God has pronounced that the princes and people have become corrupted, making them of no worth.

- *Wine mixed with water* – Wine was one of the most precious commodities due to its need for surviving in a desert place. This priceless commodity has now become diluted, mixed with the common, adulterated. In other words, the pure has mingled with the un-pure.

It doesn't take much selfishness to cause one to shy away from the responsibilities that God has commanded. Just a little dross will ruin the value of the silver and likewise just a little water can dilute the wine to a tasteless juice.

> *1 Corinthians 5:6*, *"Your glorying is not good. Know ye not that a little leaven leaveneth the whole lump?"*

How true! Just a "pinch" of self will make a giver turn to selfish acts.

Paul had a frustrated moment with the Galatian church. He found that there were some who had come to them and began to demand that they return to the old law act of circumcision. He knew full well how that this one compromise would lead to another and then to another, eventually making them turn from the knowledge and grace of God to living by Pharisaical means of law and judgments. He went as far as to call it a hindrance to obedience to truth, and, the idea of going back was not from the One who had called them, Jesus Christ their Lord!

> *Galatians 5:7-9*, *"Ye did run well; who did hinder you that ye should not obey the truth? This persuasion cometh not of him that calleth you. A little leaven leaveneth the whole lump."*

Just a "tad" of self-righteousness goes a long way. Like dropping a little garlic into a pot of soup and it changes the taste of the whole thing. And, if you keep dropping a little more of this and a little more of that, it will eventually steal away the reason for the soup in the first place.

Our focus must remain on the lost and hurting around us. When we take our eye off the ball it will be stolen from us before we have time to react.

Sin of Sodom?

If I were to ask you what the sin of Sodom was, your response would probably be the same as mine has always been...Sodomy or homosexuality...right? We should examine Ezekiel chapter 16 before we hastily answer with what we have presumed.

> *Ezekiel 16:46-50, "And your older sister is Samaria, she and her daughters who are dwelling on your left. And your younger sister from you who dwells on the right is Sodom and her daughters.Yet you have not walked in their ways nor have done according to their abominations. As if it were only a little thing, you were even more corrupted than they in all your ways. As I live, declares the Lord Jehovah, your sister Sodom, she and her daughters, have not done as you and your daughters have done. Behold, this was the iniquity of your sister Sodom: pride, fullness of bread, and abundance of idleness was in her and her daughters. Also, she did not strengthen the hand of the poor and needy. Also, they were haughty and did abomination before My face, so I turned them away as I saw fit."*

These "twin cities of sin" had no regard for humanity. The very base vices that led to abominations before God were *"pride, fullness of bread, and abundance of idleness...she did not strengthen the hand of the poor and needy."* This haughty attitude toward people eventually brought abominable acts that nauseated the God that loved them.

Sounds a whole lot like our society today!

Yet again...a little leaven will spoil the whole lump.

Be A Strength During Trials

> **Hebrews 12:11-15**, *"Now no chastening for the present seemeth to be joyous, but grievous: nevertheless afterward it yieldeth the peaceable fruit of righteousness unto them which are exercised thereby. Wherefore lift up the hands which hang down, and the feeble knees; And make straight paths for your feet, lest that which is lame*

be turned out of the way; but let it rather be healed.
Follow peace with all men, and holiness, without which
no man shall see the Lord: Looking diligently lest any
man fail of the grace of God; lest any root of bitterness
springing up trouble you, and thereby many be defiled"

The writer of Hebrews points out that trials are not pleasant when you are in the middle of the storm. He calls it "chastening", which is to inflict suffering for the purpose of moral improvement and eventual chaste lifestyle. This sinful nature will spiral downward into the depths of hideous acts if this chastening does not take place on a continuing basis. After these times of grievous experiences it will yield peaceable fruit of righteousness…note that it says, "…*unto them which are exercised thereby.*" In other words, not all will allow this process to take place. They would prefer to drown it out through any kind of distraction; sports, immoral acts, drugs or alcohol, busyness with friends, family, texting, social media, movies, or work. That list is endless. It is anything that will distract attention away from the purpose of the chastening…its results will make one better, not bitter.

Be quick to recognize when a brother or sister are being tested. The emotions will be all over the place, so it's imperative to recognize what is happening.

How should we encourage a fellow Christian during this chastening process?…"*Wherefore…*", or because of what has just been said, "…*lift up the hands which hang down, and the feeble knees; and make straight paths for your feet, lest that which is lame be turned out of the way; but let it rather be healed.*"

I can't express it enough that the onlooker, friend, or counselor must be cognizant of this affliction. That it is not fatal, nor is it something to shrug off as just a bad day. It's a time that God is attempting to cleanse out some "self" will. Recognize it and encourage to stand strong through it. Until the healing takes place.

Why is it important that we recognize and encourage? Because a soul is at stake!

Many tend to use this opportunity to become preachy or condescending. Valuable parts of the body have been lost during these times of testing because leadership has been insensitive to what was going on, and instead of gathering in close and becoming a stronger unit, it weakens the whole.

If the process isn't fulfilled in an individual's life they will either remain a weak vessel that hasn't grown, or they will become bitter and become defiled. Defiled vessels are no longer useful until they are placed in the sink and some detergent (or bleach) has been applied to clean them up and restored to usefulness.

Don't attempt to take the trial away, nor do we leave them to their own demise. Be a strength to them in their vulnerable and weakened state. Surround them, protect them, and encourage…but let the process build character in their lives.

Molting Eagles

I will not go into the depths of this process, but an eagle must go through several stages within their lifespan and the most trying is the molting stages. While they are vulnerable to predators and weakened from fatigue and do not have the ability to hunt for food during this time, the other eagles will gather around them. They will bring some fresh meat, fend off predators, and simply stand guard. They can't fix their problem, but they can be there during their problem. Why? Because they will be there some day and when they do, they too will need others to lend a helping hand.

Being there is not a cliché! It should be a practice.

CHAPTER 10

Addicts know no limits!!

> *1Corinthians 16:13-17*, *"Watch ye, stand fast in the faith, quit you like men, be strong. Let all your things be done with charity. I beseech you, brethren, (ye know the house of Stephanas, that it is the first fruits of Achaia, and that they have addicted themselves to the ministry of the saints, That ye submit yourselves unto such, and to every one that helpeth with us, and laboureth. I am glad of the coming of Stephanas and Fortunatus and Achaicus: for that which was lacking on your part they have supplied."*

It is interesting to see that the house of Stephanas was "addicted" to caring for others. Then, they are admonished to submit to such that are caring. Also notice the words "helpeth" and "laboureth". Perhaps the reason we do not pursue the avenue of caring for others, to the degree that we should, is that it is too much work. And, as leadership we have bought into the "delegation" of caring for others.

We are a selfish generation! We like our pass time hobbies. Don't cramp my style mentality has crept into the church.

We have no excuse you know. Maybe back in the 1800s or perhaps in the fifth century, but, no excuses can be used in the 20th century church. We have every communication tool possible…and who knows what else will come along down the road.

Who would have imagined having a facebook account that would connect you with old school mates, colleagues, family, and friends that you have not spoke with in twenty years or more. Remember when we only had mail? Before the first class stamp? How about pre-Pony Express days…how about before paper…before ink was invented.

I know…we cannot imagine what it would be like without our cell phones! When you need someone, you call them. Doesn't matter where you are at, just call! Remember when we had roaming charges? If you were not in the five county radios established for your cellular devise, then you paid $.25 per minute…and oh how painful that was!!

Now, we can call from just about anywhere and never incur additional charges. Or, we can Skype or Facetime!   How convenient!! We don't even have to log off or stop the conversations with a dozen others while we talk to family on the other side of the world.

Modern technology has connected us to every corner of the world!

So, what is our excuse? When someone comes to mind, why can't we call just to say hello? Or send a quick text to someone with a simple, "was just thinking about you and wanted to let you know you are in my thoughts and prayers" Why is that so hard?

With all the technology, and with trillions of texts per second and billions of cell phone calls per minute, we have a lot of conversation and not enough communication.

Addiction Defined

Addiction – "the state of being enslaved to a habit or practice or to something that is psychologically or physically habit-forming, as narcotics, to such an extent that its cessation causes severe trauma. Giving over or surrender."

It may help for us to define the addict as well…

Addict – "a person who is <u>addicted</u> to an activity, habit, or substance:

I recall a time in my life when I got hooked on a video game called "Asteroids". The player had so many space ships to his fleet and as you passed certain quantity milestones you would add more ships to the fleet, allowing you to go longer and longer. I was the asteroid king in the town in which we lived. What an accomplishment!! (just kidding)
The only way someone could get my initials off of the top 20

screen was to unplug the machine and hope I didn't show up for a day or so.

That is an addict!

Addicts are known as a devotee, fanatic, or junkie. All of these titles show the uncontrollable devotion one can find themselves wrapped up in. It can be anything that captures your attention and you are not able to turn aside until you have partaken of its devices. Good or bad!

To have an addiction, as *Stephanas*, to the ministry of the saints, you must be so consumed that when the need appears you cannot turn aside until you have gotten involved with solving the need.

Its not grandstanding, its taking action when the need presents it's self!

The addiction has a force stronger than one's self will. You cannot be talked out of it. Nor can you use psychological steps to help turn away your attention…you are an addict! You are a "ministry of the saints" junkie! A fanatic!! You are devoted to the cause of ministry.

If we could only find ourselves in this state more often than not. How we would change our world!

Fresh Burden Fall On Me!

A while back I took a trip to visit my sister and her family in Bordeaux France. She and her husband, Paul, went to Bordeaux over twenty years ago to start a work there. Almost eight hundred thousand people in the city and surrounding communities…a field needing the seed of the Gospel.

As I neared the end of my visit, the last weekend was to be spent attending the French National Convention, which was to be held in Bordeaux. As the convention approached, I found myself with some free time, so I placed some items in my backpack and took a hike down the road to a Castle called "The Castle of the Black Prince". It had intrigued me because it had a history of being a strategic location where many invasions required the intruders to attempt to take this Chateau that stood far above the river on a high bluff. There was a small passage, or street, that led up the hill to the gate of the castle which was purposely very narrow and steep. This small street was call "Street of Blood".

Several hundred years ago during one of the invasions this street literally ran with the blood of those attempting to take this castle.

As I toured the place, I found myself sitting at one high point overlooking a bridge that had a constant flow of traffic going north and south. This was a main thoroughfare from Spain northward through France and beyond, so the traffic was extremely heavy. As I watched the plethora of vehicles coming and going, I felt the nudge of the Spirit speaking to my heart. I felt God speaking to me on this wise…"Mark, in less than a second there will be more souls on this bridge than are currently in the church of Bordeaux. In under a minute there are more souls on this bridge than will be in the convention. In less than an hour more souls will pass over this bridge than are in the Church worldwide at this moment."   I began to feel the burden settling upon my heart as I ask the Lord, "Then, how can we reach them all?" I began to weep and pray for guidance and direction that day in more earnest. My conclusion, which is too simple I'm sure, was that we cannot reach them without the wind of the Holy Spirit blowing in and through our lives! We must have a book of Acts experience that will propel us to greater revival. Revival services that glean one or two here and there (not down grading the single soul that all heaven rejoices over) must not be our complete focus! Jumping from one conference to another and getting stirred, with no real change or results, cannot remain the norm. To preach the Gospel to all the World we will have to become addicted to caring for every soul.

Every single day souls are dying and going into eternity lost…who cares?

Comfort and Encouragement Brings Healing

Isaiah 35 is a chapter containing Messianic prophetic speak. Consider with me the following verses, by taking them to heart, in that, it is through our hands that Christ Jesus has his work in the earth today…

Isaiah 35:3-7, *"Strengthen ye the weak hands, and*

confirm the feeble knees. Say to them that are of a fearful heart, Be strong, fear not: behold, your God will come with vengeance, even God with a recompense; he will come and save you. Then the eyes of the blind shall be opened, and the ears of the deaf shall be unstopped. Then shall the lame man leap as an hart, and the tongue of the dumb sing: for in the wilderness shall waters break out, and streams in the desert. And the parched ground shall become a pool, and the thirsty land springs of water: in the habitation of dragons, where each lay, shall be grass with reeds and rushes."

You've heard it said, "You do your part and God will do the rest"…blind eyes will be opened, deaf ears unstopped, lame will leap, the dumb will speak, the wilderness that you have been experiencing will turn to a watered plain with plenty…if….it all hinges on you doing your part first…strengthen the weak hands, comfort the feeble knees, and encourage the fearful!

The *Hebrew* for "strengthen" refers to the strength residing in the *hand* for grasping and holding a thing. In other words, get involved! It isn't just a verbal encouragement of saying, "I'll pray for you.", but it implies that one must get involved with his hands by grasping and holding strongly. Action!

I have a friend that would be the prime example for "strengthening" those around him. His name is Mike, and I can't tell you how many times he has just shown up to help with an emergency project. Without being called upon, he will find out about a need and just goes after it until he figures out how to get it done. It is no wonder that God has blessed he and his wife! And I pray that more blessings fall upon them for their kindness.

Pleasures All Mine!

It is difficult to battle evil alone. Can it be done? Sure…through Christ who strengthens me. But, it is important to develop relationships with people who will encourage you and give you biblically sound advice. Paul shares with us the importance of caring for the needs of others…

Romans 15:1-7, *"We then that are strong ought to bear the infirmities of the weak, and not to please ourselves Let every one of us please his neighbour for his good to edification.*

81

For even Christ pleased not himself; but, as it is written, The reproaches of them that reproached thee fell on me. For whatsoever things were written aforetime were written for our learning, that we through patience and comfort of the scriptures might have hope. Now the God of patience and consolation grant you to be likeminded one toward another according to Christ Jesus: That ye may with one mind and one mouth glorify God, even the Father of our Lord Jesus Christ. Wherefore receive ye one another, as Christ also received us to the glory of God."

The pleasure received, when a person gives of themselves to others is immeasurable. It is not until years later that you find young people that you had mentored coming back and encouraging you in later years. Or family members that stop by your table in a McDonalds to let you know how they were touched by your hospital visit of a dying parent.

The pleasure is all yours!! For those who give themselves to the needs of others. Bearing the infirmities of the weak can be trying and time consuming. It is when the weak become strong and then turn and help you or others that you know that it was worth it all.

The Enemy of Caring

"Self". Self is the direct enemy of caring. They are on opposite sides of the battle lines. When a family, group, congregation, ministry, or business begins to loose their grip on caring for others, you will find selfishness as the root cause.

Selfish is "concerned excessively or exclusively with oneself: seeking or concentrating on one's own advantage, pleasure, or well-being without regard for others"

There are other words that begin with "self" that we could take a quick glance at. For instance...

- Self-absorbed is "absorbed in one's own thoughts, activities, or interests"
- Self-centered is "independent of outside force or influence, concerned solely with one's own desires, needs, or interests"

- Selflessness is "having no concern for self"

It doesn't take a lot of spirituality to figure out which of these three would be most Christ-like. But, as we call ourselves "Christian" (one who emulates Christ) we tend to steer away from being selfless.

Human nature is more powerful than Satan in this area. The enemy may use our human nature against us, but, we are our own worst enemy! My tendency is to be selfish, self-absorbed, and self-centered...far from us to be selfless.

From Blasphemy to The Peace Of God

Colossians 3:8-15, *"But now ye also put off all these; anger, wrath, malice, blasphemy, filthy communication out of your mouth. Lie not one to another, seeing that ye have put off the old man with his deeds; And have put on the new man, which is renewed in knowledge after the image of him that created him: Where there is neither Greek nor Jew, circumcision nor uncircumcision, Barbarian, Scythian, bond nor free: but Christ is all, and in all. Put on therefore, as the elect of God, holy and beloved, bowels of mercies, kindness, humbleness of mind, meekness, longsuffering; Forbearing one another, and forgiving one another, if any man have a quarrel against any: even as Christ forgave you, so also do ye. And above all these things put on charity, which is the bond of perfectness. And let the peace of God rule in your hearts, to the which also ye are called in one body; and be ye thankful."*

I always understood "blasphemy" to be related to what we do against the Holy Spirit. Honestly, it was something that we held over our head even though we could not completely explain it. We just knew it was bad and we shouldn't do it. I've heard many attempts to explain blasphemy against the Holy Ghost...most of which just didn't seem to make complete sense.

One morning while reading the above scripture the thought struck me that the term "blasphemy" just didn't fit with the other verbs listed. Anger, wrath, malice, and filthy communication just didn't have anything to do with "something" we did against

83

God. So, as usual, my curiosity led me to seek out the definitions and further understand the context of the word "blasphemy".

Blasphemy is drawn from the Greek word "bema" (bay-ma), which has its base from a word that means "step or foot breath" or a "rostrum" (pulpit?). The more applicable definitions would be "tribunal, judgment seat, set foot on, throne".

If I take these translations and boil it down to a level that I can absorb, I begin to understand that God is telling us that we cannot sit on the throne of judgment, which is the basis for all the emotions and reactions stated in the rest of the verse.

Blasphemy is used here in a relational context, in that all the "put off all these" has to do with our relationship with people. "Lie not one to another" is just as filthy as the "filthy communication" that we thump our pulpits with.

This passage is an attempt to show the true nature of humanity! It comes natural to be sneaky and conniving, in an attempt to get our way. Our view is birth place and status…Greek, Jew, Barbarian, Scythian…if I can modernize this…Getto, Country Boy, City Slicker, and so forth.

The shift what we need to "put off" to what we need to "put on" contrasts one another. One comes natural…the other requires effort. Even down to forgiving a fellow of a wrong doing. It all requires various levels of work on our part. Just like prayer, fasting, reading the Scriptures…disciplines that are habit forming once we make the conscience effort to move away from the things we need to "put off" to the things we need to "put on".

Some are good a "Putting On" but fewer are able to be the real deal. It isn't until we meet adversity that we are exposed to the "putting on" or have "put on" the attributes of Christ. When you are the top dog it easy to hide our sins.

All of the attributes that are listed bring us to the primary thought…"let the peace of God rule in your hearts". It is in the "put off" and the "put on" that will determine if peace will rule in our hearts. It challenges us to move from blasphemy, and those human attitudes that are related to how we truly feel about others, to peace in our hearts by putting on mercy, kindness, humbleness of mind….

Compassion Compels One To Care

> *Mark 8:1-3, "In those days the multitude being very great, and having nothing to eat, Jesus called his disciples unto him, and saith unto them, I have compassion on the multitude, because they have now been with me three days, and have nothing to eat: And if I send them away fasting to their own houses, they will faint by the way: for divers of them came from far."*

Time and time again, Jesus healed the lame, the sick, and even the hungry. He was moved with compassion for them over and over again.

Compassion compels us to care about the needs. It is unfortunate that there is more concern for a beached dolphin than there is for a saint of God who has gone astray. Compassion…where is it? We must be moved by it! It is a powerful force!!

I just wonder if we were actually filled with compassion if we would not see more healings, miracles, signs and wonders. Not that it is in our own ability to do these things, but rather that God is moved when we are moved in the right way.

Our lacking of empathy has made us spiritually pathetic.

Sure, we feel sorry for those going through the storm, but truth be told we are just glad it isn't "me". So, we say, "I'll pray for you…" and as soon as we walk away that sorry feeling has moved on to bigger and better entertainment.

Compassion drove the Master to fix the problem. We should look at a few examples:

> *Matt. 14:14 – And Jesus went forth, and saw a great multitude, and was moved with **compassion** toward them, and he healed their sick.*

> *Mark 1:40,41 – And there came a leper…And Jesus,*

85

> *moved with **compassion**, put forth his hand, and <u>touched him</u>, and saith unto him, "I will; be thou clean"*
>
> ***Matt. 15:32*** *– Then Jesus called his disciples unot him, and said, "I have **compassion** on the multitude…I will not send them away fasting, lest they faint in the way"*
>
> ***Luke 7:13*** *– And when the Lord saw her, he had **compassion** on her, and said unto her, "Weep not".*

Even his parables contained the same theme…

> ***Matt. 18:27*** *– "Then the lord of that servant was moved with **compassion**, and loosed him, and forgave him the debt."*
>
> ***Luke 10:33*** *– "But when a <u>certain</u> Samaritan, as he journeyed, came where he was; and when he saw him, he had **compassion** on him"*
>
> ***Luke 15:20*** *– "And he arose, and came to his father. But when he was yet a great way off, his father saw him, and had **compassion**, and ran, and fell on his neck, and kissed him."*

Compassion – "Deep awareness of the suffering of another coupled with the wish to relieve it"

What kind of revival would we have if we could simply be moved with compassion for the needs of those around us…

<u>Songs Turn To Wailing</u>

The Lord shows the prophet Amos a basket of "summer fruit" to illustrate that there may be a sense of comfort now but the time is quickly coming that a season of destruction was to come. In chapter eight verse three, the Lord tells Amos that the joyful sounds of songs will soon turn to wailing because of their iniquity.

What would cause God to be so angry? Once again it boils down to two attitudes; 1) toward God, 2) toward humanity. I cannot get away from how focused God is on the way we treat people.

> *Amos 8:4-6*, *"Hear this, O ye that swallow up the needy, even to make the poor of the land to fail, Saying, When will the new moon be gone, that we may sell corn? and the sabbath, that we may set forth wheat, making the ephah small, and the shekel great, and falsifying the balances by deceit? That we may buy the poor for silver, and the needy for a pair of shoes; yea, and sell the refuse of the wheat?"*

The Children of Israel are reprimanded for taking advantage of the poor and needy. Serious repercussions are warned for their greed.

We find God speaking through the prophet concerning matters of the heart. Attitudes that are hid in the heart are being revealed! The Sabbath is kept with hidden reluctance. They grumbled all the way to "church", texting, making phone calls, and wishing they had left their shop open on the holiest of days. Think of all the cash that is being missed by closing the doors until after church…if we could only "do" this religious stuff and still keep the money flowing in…think of all the churches we could build…oops, I mean how many vacations could be taken…if we would just catch some of this Sabbath day traffic.

Merchandising the Gospel is a dangerous mission! The enemy of our soul will conjure up every imaginable way to entice by catering to the greedy hearts of man. Sending delusions to make merriment truth, and in the mean time throwing out truth to the dogs.

The acceptable way of doing business was for the scales to be fudged. Enticing the needy to buy cheap shoes that are substandard, offering overtime pay on weekends that draw away from family and time to worship, and tipping the scales with their toe when no one is looking.

Jehovah God was wroth with the greed, lack of concern for the things of God, and the hidden motives behind it all.
Consider with me this thought. Would any church or congregation have any concern about what is being sung, or problems with having to pump the crowd like a high school pep rally, if miracles, signs, and wonders were happening every day?

I don't think so!

It appears to me that we are continually trying to "bring down" the presence of God by finding the right combination of beat, lyrics, and mood for each weekend service. All the while we wrestle and struggle with frustrations because "nothings happening". Perhaps it is time to lay aside weights that have crept into our religious lifestyle.

Before any of us get all defensive or indignant let us consider the fact that the Book of Acts recorded much rejoicing. They went from house to house breaking bread in fellowship, going up daily to the temple, seeking peace with all men, and following the leading of the Holy Spirit. Prayer and supplication was as natural as eating three balanced meals each day. Speaking of their beloved Messiah was continually on their lips. They sought out the poor, needy, lame, sickly, blind, and even the dead to see what God would do for them! And, when the Scriptures recorded a gathering it was accompanied by great rejoicing, conversions by the thousands, and the Gospel spread like wild fire to the four corners of the known world.

Contrast that with where we are today…

Those early believers were addicted to caring for the needs of others, just as Jesus was. From the physical to the spiritual well being of everyone that would hear them. This excitement brought a move of the Spirit and fanned the fires of revival to go before them in every burg, hamlet, and city they went to.

Get addicted to caring and see what God will do!!

CHAPTER 11

How Did Jesus Die?

I had a Bible College friend loose his son in an accident, and I recall the feelings that overwhelmed me on their behalf. I had been going through a tough time, but, it reminded me that life brings challenges our way that are, in our own ability, too much to bear on our own.

After a couple days, I felt inclined to encourage my friend and just send a note from time to time, just to let him know that I was thinking of him. At first, he seemed to respond very well, but it didn't take long for the pain to surface and I had to back off for a period of time. I can't say that I did it willingly…due to my own circumstances I wanted to help bring healing to this couple's life and I continued to push for a while until I felt the sting of a couple responses that let me know that I needed to give them some space.

Several months went by and one day I received a call from this friend. I was in shock at first, and then I felt the flood of emotions as we began to talk through some of his time of healing. I immediately apologized for anything that I may have said or done, and began to explain that I wanted to help so desperately. His affirmation came back with explanations that I hadn't said anything wrong it was just that he had closed down and was striking out at everyone…even those who tried to help. Unfortunately, as he shared, there were those who did step over their boundaries and said things that only added to their pain. So, even though my attempts to encourage were correctly administered, the other circumstances had affected his ability to receive from me as well.

As the discussion moved along, this friend shared that one positive turning point was when an individual called and felt led to ask him the question, "Why did Jesus die?", and the quick response was, "For our sin!". The person then asked, "No. How did Jesus die?", and the immediate retort was "We all know it was for the sins of the world." The caller then explained, "No. He died of a broken heart. His heart broke and bleed for your broken heart. For God knows the broken feeling that is tearing your heart apart, and he died with a broken heart for your brokenness."

My friend immediately began to feel the healing power of God as he realized that yes, he was literally dying of a broken heart, and it took a man with boldness, yet a humble and contrite spirit, to come to him and help identify the root of the problem. This broken heart was literally killing my friend and draining him little by little…day by day…to the point that his wife would wake up at night just to make sure he was still breathing.

I share this story because it helps me keep in perspective that even the most caring individual can make a mess of a situation when they attempt to help without the leading of the Holy Ghost. Yes, we need to reach out to them. Yes, we need to be there through the bad times. But, there comes a point to which the person's heart is breaking and they are dying physically and spiritually…and it will require much prayer and anointing to reach out and to heal at the right time.

Jesus died of a broken heart…why?...because he cares for what we are facing in this life. He cares that our very life is being sucked out of us because the situations have become insurmountable. In our human ability, and even with a knowledge of God through the Holy Spirit, we cannot heal a heart that is braking into tiny pieces. Never to be repaired if God does not intervene!

Remember Humpty Dumpty? Though a cute little children's story, the concept can be applied to a heart that is broken down by the pain that life throws our way. All the kings horses and men couldn't begin to put this kind of spiritual, psychological, and physical breakdown back together. The cracks in the armor are too deep and only the One that was broken for us, could ever bring the correct healing balm that is needed.

Jesus died of a broken heart for the broken hearted!

I Can't Complain

> This spiritual song explains my guiding light…

I've had some good days
I've had some hills to climb
I've had some weary days
I've had some weary nights
But when I look around
And think things over
All of my good days
They outweigh my bad days

So I can't complain

Sometimes my clouds hang low
I ask the Lord to see them go
And then I ask the question
Lord why so much pain
But God knows what's best for me
Although my weary, weary eyes can't see

So I'll say thank you Lord
I can't complain

God's been so good to me
The Lord has been so good to me
More than this world could ever be
The Lord has been so good to me
And he dried my tears away
And he turn all my midnights he turned them all into day

So I'll say thank you Lord
I just say thank you Lord
I'll just say thank you Lord
I can't complain

I believe the redeemed of the Lord should be able to sing that song…through every circumstance that life blasts us with.

Boundaries and Grey Areas

"A picture is worth a thousand words", so let me attempt to start with drawing a word picture to illustrate a further point.

When visiting a rancher friend in South Dakota, we had the fun of trying to separate his herd from a neighbor's herd. That summer had been extremely wet so the tanks (small natural ponds in low areas) were up by several feet. Any time a border went through one of these tanks the fence would disappear several yards out in the water and then reappear directly on the opposite end of the tank. As any country boy knows, animals have a natural instinct to be herdy…in other words, if you have two pastures coming together and the animals can touch noses, they will eventually find a way to get together. So, a double hot wire fence may be needed or a single wire set back a few feet from the barb wire border fence will keep them from sticking their nose across.

As a friend told me once, you don't plant crops close enough to a fence where a cow can be tempted to push through the fence, otherwise the temptation is greater than the fence can restrain.

On this particular day, the cows looked across this pond, where the fence had disappeared under the surface and the boundary restraints were unclear, they looked over and saw cows from the neighbor's herd and instinctively felt that they should be over there as well. Before it was all said and done they had a couple hundred cows that had to be separated. It took several 4-wheelers and a pick up truck, opening gates, and a lot of energy to get everyone back into the proper pastures.

I mention this so that we can see that simply slapping up a single wire fence may work in an isolated environment but when temptation increases, greater restraint is needed to keep from wasting time and energy, as well as embarrassment with neighbors.

As we continue to cultivate a more caring spirit I would want to add an additional "wire" of restraint to our temptation to take this thought and assume that every situation will require us to run to the aide of a person without any regard to what is transpiring in that individuals life.

Restraints In Caring For Others

Following is a short list of restraints that we should consider:

Gender – reaching to the opposite sex can be fatal.
Physical harm – some situations must be approached with

caution.

Rebellion – enablement is when we cater to someone with best of intentions to help.

History of conflict – when you've been there and it seems to have aggravated the situation.

Chemical abuse – support as a friend but encourage professional help.

Sympathy Card – when drawn into a situation only for the sake of being sympathetic

Give Space but not abandon – It is ok to give space to one that strikes out at your hand of kindness, but it isn't an occasion to abandon reaching all together.

There is a slippery slope any time you see someone faltering and you wish to help. It takes much more prayer than words. If your time of prayer isn't at least two to one, then wait till you can pray. Seek God's direction and guidance for the situation.

It isn't always for you to solve...just show you care about them as a person and friend.

Balance Is Needed

In our reaching out to others, there will be those who are so wounded that they are like a caged animal. Not knowing who is their friend or foe, they will strike out at any attempt to help. During those times it seems that anything said is taken wrong or perceived as another strike against them. Remember that it is a challenging time for them, and for those that care. It will require much prayer for wisdom, and a very gentle, slow, but deliberant approach...and, you may get a few scratches and scars from the retaliation...but, it may save a soul.

If you are the one in the "cage"...keep in mind that when people reach to you, even though they may not say the right things all the time, it hurts when you reject the caring hand of kindness. Allow those who try to help a little room for mistakes as well. Very few, if any, have a silver tongue that can say all the right things at the absolute right time. Well meaning people can be the most destructive, it seems, but, at least they are trying!

Care to Bear

Need I remind us of **Romans 15:1**? It says, *"We then that are strong ought to bear the infirmities of the weak, and not to please ourselves."*

I find, as I do some introspecting, that the tendency is for the strong to step on the weak. Shun those that are feeble. But to bear the infirmities of the weak? Who preaches that kind of selflessness anymore?

Infirmity literally means, in this context, a scruple of conscience. Those that do not have all their mental faculties working. The elevator does not go to the top floor. A brick shy of a full load. A spoon shy of a full setting. All of these insensitive applications show how that we really view those that are less fortunate.

In a broader sense, I believe this Scripture is encouraging a humble spirit to grip us at any point where we feel superior to our brother. I don't feel, based on the many Scriptures we have discussed, that God has limited this command to "bear" up those that are weak. But, in fact, His intent is to be a reminder that any time we feel we have the trump card in hand that we should immediately do that which does not "please ourselves". Take the low road in every situation.

If the strong would do this every time we feel a surge of superior strength, it would destroy the enemies devices! Instead, when we have an advantage we grab it and shake the diploma in the face of others to insure they know who is boss. Advantage is the destroyer of peace in a community of believers. Once a person begins to abuse their God given advantage to insure their will is accomplished, it will destroy love, hope, and peace in all that follow.

Prayer Requests

> **James 5:13-14**, *"Is any among you afflicted? let him pray. Is any merry? let him sing psalms. Is any sick among you? let him call for the elders of the church; and let them pray over him, anointing him with oil in the name of the Lord."*

"Afflicted" is defined as follows: to undergo hardship: be afflicted, endure afflictions (hardness), suffer trouble.

An affliction isn't just a physical ailment. It can be depression, financial struggles, unwanted breakups or divorce, addictions, persecution, home life, and church dissention… just to name a few.

It shouldn't be viewed as a negative when God takes, or allows, us to go through a time of affliction. For, it will cause us to pray more fervently to seek the face of God so that we can understand His will and purpose for this situation.

But then we look further at this passage to find that there is a balance that is needed where we need the encouragement of others…

"Sick", as found in verse 14, can be interpreted as: to be feeble (in any sense), be diseased, impotent folk, sick, or weak.

This simple definition implies that when a person is feeble or weak, then it is time for the body to come to their aid. The diseased or impotent are in need of faith building prayer from those who are strong.

If you have become wore out by the fight, you need the strength of others!

I believe I am correct in this interpretation because in verse 15 we find the word "sick" again but this time it brings additional clarification for that which is being prayed for.

> **James 4:15,** *"And the prayer of faith shall save the sick, and the Lord shall raise him up.."*

"Sick" in this passage has a different definition…to *toil*, to *tire*, be faint, sicken, be wearied.

The prayer of faith will save the wearied…those who have become faint. This requires a group effort…the body working together…bearing up the weak.

I find it ironic that the Scriptures repeat over and over that we should strengthen one another, yet, instead we run to our corner and gaze at those who are afflicted by the enemy and watch them lie in anguish, as if it were a matinee at the movies. Taking bets as to how many more breaths they will take before the "sick" finally expire.

Boston Marathon Bombing (April 2013)

As so many of us, the Boston Marathon bombing was a shock. To those that were on the scene, it was immediate mayhem. Innocent children who came to watch their dad or mom run a marathon that was historic in their lives, only to have tragic consequences for being at the wrong place at the wrong time.

As the explosions shook the area close to the finish line, most began to run away from the scene in fear, while a handful of ordinary citizens ran to the aid of hurting.

Carlos came only to honor his deceased son who was killed in Iraq, yet when others needed help he left his agenda and aided the hurting.

Allan came for a completely different reason, which was to see his wife run in the marathon, only to find himself in the chaos helping people that were hurt on the scene.

Both, though from different worlds on a social scale, were not inclined to run from danger when they saw the pain inflicted to others. They were drawn with compassion to help the hurting.

We have lost focus of the fact that God is moved with compassion for every human being! And it is our responsibility to view them as God does.

Pride will continue to remain the primary enemy to seeing a complete body. We are encouraged to *"Confess your faults one to another, and pray one for another, that ye may be healed."* (James 5:16)

Confess your faults? That doesn't compute with our current structure. Confession is for the weak and the outright sinner! Not for those of us who have no fault! Oh how we have missed the boat…it has sailed from the harbor and we are left behind!

"Faults" is defined as; a *side slip*, unintentional *error,* or even a willful *transgression.*

Who hasn't been there? Only the Pharisee will say they have not. We've all sinned and come short of the glory of God. If nothing more than a "side slip", which is a lapse or deviation, from what God would have for us to do or be.

The admonishment continues by saying that the response should be that we pray one for another, that ye may be healed. How we need that kind of healing in our midst!!

Only those who have cultivated a culture of caring will go to this kind of extreme. We do not like to make ourselves vulnerable by admitting any guilt. We have assumed the throne of God to be our own when we do not confess our faults. That is a dangerous place to assume…just ask Lucifer if you do not think so.

Check Your Spirit

There is nothing new that has not happened in times past…

> ***Ecclesiastes 1:9-11,*** *"The thing that hath been, it is that which shall be; and that which is done is that which shall be done: and there is no new thing under the sun. Is there any thing whereof it may be said, See, this is new? it hath been already of old time, which was before us. There is no remembrance of former things; neither shall there be any remembrance of things that are to come with those that shall come after."*

We tend to forget that the same challenges have been going on for thousands of years. The same human nature rises up in us that has risen up in the hearts of men since Cain killed Abel with a rock. (Interesting to note that God cursed mankind with having to toil and move the very rock that Cain ended up using. Perhaps the pre-meditation came from days of cursing God for having to work…)

The greatest enemy of caring…our spirit.

There was a man who started out with humility. He hid when

97

others promoted him. He followed Godly instructions and worshipped God for his guidance. But, over time, his position became his focus. He worked more to protect his own interests than pursuing God's heart. It eventually became his, and his children's, demise. This man was King Saul.

Human nature can rise up and destroy with such subtlety that one does not even realize its existence. It blinds so that we cannot see the hand of God at work in other's lives.

When David received some praise, and Saul could see that God had blessed David, it dug down into his spirit. Evil caused Saul to "prophesy" against David…I can only imagine what that prophesy sounded like! "I will smite David even to the wall…"

It is important that we keep a check valve on our spirit. Any time we begin to feel the urge to destroy the reputation of an individual, we have allowed the human nature to rise up and work its way into our spirit. The only remedy is a repentant heart! Quickly falling on our knees and asking God to help us.

We can't buck against God's favor. No matter how disturbing it may be to us. Even if they have done us wrong, we must rely on the all knowing, all seeing, all powerful will and purpose of God!

Don't Mess With Texas?

You've heard the slogan, "Don't mess with Texas!" Well, I have one better than that…"Don't mess with the apple of God's eye!"

> ***Zechariah 2:8,*** *"For thus saith the LORD of hosts; After the glory hath he sent me unto the nations which spoiled you: for he that toucheth you toucheth the apple of his eye."*

Favoritism is only allowed when you are God! The key is staying in such a way that you are considered the "apple of his eye".

When an object is thrown at you the immediate reaction is to duck or throw up a hand to protect the eyes. I wonder if God will tend to immediately respond with the same protective gesture to protect the "apple of his eye".

God will protect His own! You can trust in that!!

The King Is Taking Note

I would remind us of the parable that Jesus, as the King, gave a dividing line based on the acts of kindness shown to the hungry, thirsty, strangers, naked, sick, and imprisoned. These kind gestures had eternal rewards. The have and have not's were defined by those that fed, gave, took in, clothed, or came to the rescue of those in need…or those that didn't.

> *Matthew 25:37-40, "Then shall the righteous answer him, saying, Lord, when saw we thee an hungered, and fed thee? or thirsty, and gave thee drink? When saw we thee a stranger, and took thee in? or naked, and clothed thee? Or when saw we thee sick, or in prison, and came unto thee? And the King shall answer and say unto them, Verily I say unto you, Inasmuch as ye have done it unto one of the least of these my brethren, ye have done it unto me."*

The "righteous" were so involved with their positive behavior that they had to ask when they did any of these for the King. Those that were cast out into darkness were never aware of the needs around them. Too busy? Too much partying? Selfish? Or just caught up with restoring a car, fishing, or playing golf.

The endless list of things that can occupy our focus and time will seem so trivial when we stand before the King of kings and attempt to excuse the fact that we simply didn't care enough to notice the needs of others.

As my dad says, "Too heavenly minded to be of any earthly good.", could apply to so many Christians.

It takes cultivating…remember, the act of enhancing the soil to maximize the production. We have to dig around in places that we have allowed to get packed down. Not that it was intentional! Just the rain of blessings, wind of adversity, and the heat of a sun that beat down on a hot summers day all combined to cause a crust that doesn't allow the fruits to come forth.

One challenge that a farmer will have in the spring planting season is when they work the ground and plant just before a hard rain that is followed by a couple of warm days. The rain packs the dirt above the seed, and then the warm sun rays will bake the mud into a thin layer of crust that will not allow the kernel to germinate and push through. Attention to the weather patterns is crucial. When the risk is taken and on the short end, then the hoe is needed to break up the crust.

Take some time to ask God for direction in how to reach out to the hurting around you. Boy's and girl's clubs need honest Christians to be an example. Big Brother / Big Sister type organizations need Holy Ghost filled Saints to get involved. Senior Citizen groups and homes need volunteers that love God and people! Prison and addiction ministries are awaiting the redeemed to say so. Hospitals need volunteers to be moved with compassion for the hurting.

Fellow Christians that have stumbled or have been abandoned need you today!

What would God have you to do?

CHAPTER 12

"Sad report is we restore cars….not people" was the response to a text I had sent out to many of my pastor friends concerning the subject of restoration. It summed up the thought as well as anything I could have said.

Why is it that we are more concerned about our material possessions than the one thing that is eternal?

First Responder

As I've watched the search for almost a week, at the time of this writing, for Malaysian Flight 320, I am amazed and humbled at the extent of energy that the world is putting into finding 239 souls. Some could have been terrorists, businessmen and simple family members alike; all walks of life are represented. Multiple countries had people on this flight…yet what amazes me the most is the resources that pulled together to make sense of the disappearance of an airplane. If that were all…a large hunk of metal the expense would not make sense at all. But we are talking about 239 souls!

Emergency First Responders are instructed to stabilize and account for all human life first. That is first and foremost in their minds…before concerning themselves with the debris from the wreckage….make sure every person is attended to…FIRST!

As I rolled to my final destination in Lemont IL I came upon a wreck. The slushy snow had made the roads hazardous and the accident blocked the intersection in which I was to turn to reach the plant I was to visit. As I passed, along with the other traffic, I caught a glimpse of emergency people loading a couple of people onto stretchers and loading them into an ambulance. I had to circle a couple of miles out of my way but when I finished my appointment almost two hours later they were just finishing cleaning up the wreck. What an inconvenience for all involved….so why didn't they just ignore the two or three people involved and clean up the mess first, and let those that had made the mess worry about themselves.

That would be absurd…right? Yet, we "religious" do it all the time. The soul and the damage to human life isn't as important to most folks when a person falls, or is the victim of other's "accident".

We tend to try and protect our system first, not the souls involved.

At the very same time the news had been reporting an explosion in New York City, and the first thing they reported was a confirmation of those that had met their demise and several others that were missing. The initial wasn't the damage done to the building but rather the lives that were affected.

If our messed up media can concern themselves with people first, why can't we? I believe it will be an indictment against us when we stand before a Judge that loved humanity, and it is revealed that our tendency was to ostracize and abandon the people affected. Whether the person was the root cause of the situation or not, we must spend more energy restoring lives than cutting the losses and restoring our system.

The ironic observation has been that those who have been the recipients of much mercy and restoration have been some of the quickest to judge others. May we never forget that when much is given, much is required. It is sad when family, friends, and close acquaintances have stood behind an individual, to restore them, yet once their feet are back on solid ground, they tend to judge quickly and harshly. Let us not forget the servant that was forgiven of much and he couldn't forgive the miniscule debts owed to him…he eventually found himself thrown into a prison for this action.

I am convinced that to cultivate a culture of caring we must be more apt to go to a person and restore them…considering ourselves and our own failures first. If it were not for the Lord, where would I be??

"Many believe in forgiveness...most do NOT believe in restoration....they believe in REMODELING...making the person fit their idea of what God can do with them once they have "fallen"." ~ Curtis Riggen

Galatians 6:1-3, *"Brethren, if a man be overtaken in a fault, ye which are spiritual, restore such an one in the spirit of meekness; considering thyself, lest thou also be tempted. Bear ye one another's burdens, and so fulfil the law of Christ. For if a man think himself to be something, when he is nothing, he deceiveth himself."*

First, let's look at the term *"Brethren"*. This expression brings all that will listen to the same table. There are no "Big I's and Little You's" in the word Brethren. It levels the playing field for all. "Brethren", reminds that though we have differences or faults we are all in one family, and that "blood" runs thicker than water. It shows a certain tone of kindness, and attempts to make the following admonitions tender in nature. It also shows the status of us all..."Brethren" in the family of God.

Then we look at *"...if a man be overtaken"*. *Foremost, put yourself in the place of "man". If "Mark...be over taken"...or, Tom, Jane, or Doug...if a person be overcome with a fault. One commentary warned that "...often he who is first to find fault, is the very one who has first transgressed." The "if" begins the process of identifying one who has the over powering urge to find fault, then the instructions will be how to handle such faultiness.*

Next, we look at *"...a fault..."*. Transgression or a fall, meaning, to fall back into legal bondage. We are not just talking about a little "white lie" here, we are talking about someone that has transgressed the laws of God and have been caught in the act. What should we do with these? Throw them aside, kick em while they are down? Dog pile on them...

The caveat..."...*ye which are spiritual...*". Perhaps our greatest challenge is the "spiritual" part. Especially when we all believe we are spiritual giants. If we look at the context, leading up to this verse, we find that Paul has just outlined the sins of the flesh that need to be removed and replaced by the fruits that come from the Holy Spirit in our lives.

Without the fruits of the Spirit at work, we will not respond as one who is spiritual.

Romans 15:1, *"We then that are strong ought to bear the*

103

Perhaps our greatest challenge in laity and leadership alike is spiritual strength. We've attempted to lay down all the sins of the flesh but have not let go of the flesh, allowing the fruits of the Spirit to do their work in us without hesitation. We still like our flesh…

"…restore"! Restoration can be visualized as one who has broken a limb and a doctor would care, to the best of his ability, to heal the wound and make it as it were prior to the injury.

The warnings flashed across the screen…"WARNING: FOLLOWING VIDEO IS GRAPHIC"…as the news sped across the nation. One of the most talked about news blips for days and weeks to follow! Louisville's guard, Kevin Ware tragically injured his right leg during the Midwest Regional finals in the NCAA tournament. When the injury occurred, players immediately went to his aid, referees ran to help, medical personnel went into action, fans from both sides fell silent, while the whole sports world stopped in concern for a player that fell victim to circumstances.

Louisville went on to win the National Championship after Ware told his teammates "Win this game, win this game…" as they wheeled him out of the stadium.

What would have happened if at that point the team would have shoved Kevin out the door and said, "You're not good enough or able to be on this team any longer"? We would have called them all kinds of names, the least graphic being "stupid". No one in their right mind would have left him laying on the floor to himself and just kept on playing the ball game! Not on your life!! Teammates swarmed him, fans from every college team in the nation were concerned, and doctors rushed in to set the bones and do all they could to restore.

Although it will take a while, the good news is that they fully expect Kevin to play on the team the very next year. Sure, it will take a little time to heal and get back in game shape to play, but, that is restoration!

Taking a car that has been beaten, rusted, and damaged beyond recognition and restoring it to its original state is the goal of restoration!

This whole restoration business is not what our flesh desires. Why? Because it is easier to judge harshly until we too have fallen into sin. In most cases, personal sin isn't even the cause. Many are simply caught in the torrid currents of life and as an innocent bystander we've lost our marriage, family, and ministry...yet, those closest to us find it easier to throw the individual away instead of caring to restore.

The reaping and sowing process frustrates us, yet we seem to think we are smarter or better than we are. The Scripture admonishes to pursue restoration with *"...the spirit of meekness"*. The response is not restoration because it first requires meekness. It is one fruit that we all have problems with! Meekness is that temperament that accepts God's dealings without disputing, and so, we endure meekly His will.

Paul goes on to warn that we are to *"...consider thyself"*. Notice the singularity. Too often we consider "the church" but fail to consider (inspect) our own motives or the potential of our own ability to fall. The Pharisee would say, "I have no sin" and sit on the lofty seat of judge and jury.

And, the warning that *"...thou also be tempted.."*. *This alone should convince us to be more compassionate! An example of restoration, because there may come a day that I will need to be restored. The problem is that we really do not believe we can fail! And, when we do, the tendency is to cover our tracks or blame everyone else.*

Note that the Jewish people had the tendency to become most severe in their judgment of any weaknesses. Those that could not live the law were weak! Galatians 6:1 is somewhat of a metaphor showing that goodness and good gifts only come from God.

"Brethren, if a man be overtaken in any fault - By surprise, ignorance, or stress of temptation. *Ye who are spiritual* - Who continue to live and walk by the Spirit. *Restore such an one* - By reproof, instruction, or exhortation. *Every one who can, ought to help herein; only in the spirit of meekness* - This is essential to a spiritual man; and in this lies the whole force of the cure. **Considering thyself -** The plural is beautifully changed into the singular. **Let each take heed to himself. Lest thou also be tempted -** Temptation easily and swiftly passes from one to another; especially if a man endeavors to cure another without preserving his own meekness."

"Not everything that is faced can be changed. But, nothing can be changed until it is faced" ~ James Baldwin

Considering is a verb meaning *to look attentively*; to fix the attention upon a thing with an interest in it or to give attention in order to obtain it. Similar to how a hunter would have all his senses tuned into the hunt, especially when he has the prey in his sights.

Our attention to the need of a brother is intensified when we hone in on the areas that we are vulnerable.

Remember, the theme in verses surrounding Galatians chapter six has been by love serve one another. We are taught to deal tenderly for those who have been "overtaken in a fault".

Tenderly doesn't mean to abandon! If abandonment is a tender way of dealing with people then that would explain why parents would leave their children in a hot car or drop off their parents at a nursing home and never return. To respond in a tender way you have to get involved.

The original word, *Katartizete*, signifies to set a dislocated joint. That is our purpose! Set the disjointed lives…it may take all the kings horses and men, but, all hands on deck to restore Humpty Dumpty!!

When was the last time you felt inclined to take a burden from another's back and carry it for them? If we are directed to "bear one another's burdens", then why do we not seek out those that we can do just that? I do not believe it is saying fix their burden…bear it! Meaning, lift if from them and walk an extra mile with them so that their load is lighter and their strength is restored to go on a little further. Sure, they may have bit off more than they could chew by taking on more than they should have, but, its not for me to judge how much they should have brought with them! I'm told to bear it, not share it.

BWCA

When we took a trip to the Boundery Waters, in Northern
Minnesota, we paddled our canoes for three and a half hours and
portaged three times. Each time we had to pull everything out of
the canoes, not one person told another that they brought too
much junk! We helped one another carry everything over, then
we crawled back into our canoes and paddled to the next
portage…and eventual destination. There were some things that
we could have left back home, and I learned that lesson by the
time we had to carry it in and back out. The experience helped
me to know what to take the next time…and guaranteed it would
be less stuff on the next trip! Things I thought were a must have,
became less necessary after carrying it over a total of six
portages.

The laws of love will compel to forbear, forgive, have
compassion on the weaknesses and folly of others. Jesus came
to bear our infirmities…even our sin…and he is our example.
When a minister hands a friend his ministerial license, he is
reaching for someone to love him back to health. When a
person's world crashes down around them and they are on the
verge of a complete breakdown, the last thing they are reaching
for is phantom friendships that slip away like a bad dream.

I've known a few restorers. They are esteemed much higher
than those that have followed all protocol, ratted out for the sake
of self preservation, and built themselves up by tearing down
others. The few that seek to restore have loyal friends and
comrades that will fight for them down the road. Self-conceit is
truly self-deceit.

> *Philippians 2:1-7,* "*If there be therefore any consolation
> in Christ, if any comfort of love, if any fellowship of the
> Spirit, if any bowels and mercies, Fulfill ye my joy, that
> ye be likeminded, having the same love, being of one
> accord, of one mind. Let nothing be done through strife
> or vainglory; but in lowliness of mind let each esteem
> other better than themselves. Look not every man on his
> own things, but every man also on the things of others.
> Let this mind be in you, which was also in Christ Jesus:*

Who, being in the form of God, thought it not robbery to be equal with God: But made himself of no reputation, and took upon him the form of a servant, and was made in the likeness of men"

This is our example…and the will of God…that we follow the pattern set forth by Jesus the Christ. Though he was God, the Father of all creation, manifested in flesh…redeeming mankind back to himself, yet he exemplified the attitude lowliness. He esteemed our lives better than himself by pouring out his life's blood for those who rejected him.

I must admit that it is a continual challenge to be like my Lord. It requires repentance multiple times per day. Without the leading, and my continual humble submission, of the Holy Spirit I can never esteem others better than myself. That is anti-flesh…

Remember, 1 Corinthians 13 speaks of charity…God's way…and it is not puffed up, nor does it lift it's self above others. Charity, or love, will keep us humble.

There are no people more uncharitable than religious people who delight in having more enlightenment on Scripture. Many seem to feel they commune with God in some higher plane than everyone else. Just as Samson felt evincible with the strength that came from Yahweh, it wasn't until he found himself without his hair that he regarded the things of God in a truer light.

Act of Restoration

Genesis 43:30, "And Joseph made haste; for his bowels did yearn upon his brother: and he sought where to weep; and he entered into his chamber, and wept there"

What a beautiful example of how one will struggle with restoration. The process that Joseph went through of first forgiving his brethren, and going to his chamber and weeping over the situation I'm sure had mixed emotions.

Consider the fact that though Joseph was struggling with his own emotions, his brethren were confused by his actions. Joseph used trickery (sounds like his daddy, Jacob, the supplanter) to keep the situation in his control, until he could sort through his emotional upheaval.

It wasn't until Joseph exposed himself, in a public setting, that his brethren could finally begin the process of closure as well.

> **Genesis 45:14-15,** *"And he fell upon his brother Benjamin's neck, and wept; and Benjamin wept upon his neck. Moreover he kissed all his brethren, and wept upon them: and after that his brethren talked with him."*

Notice the phrase…*"after that his brethren talked with him."* I just wonder what was said once Joseph made his true identity known to them. Perhaps there was some repentance, some words of healing, many tears…but, we also must realize that it didn't happen until God's will was fulfilled as well.

As long as Joseph stayed in his chamber weeping, restoration was never made with his brethren. Some things have to be loud enough for the public to hear and know that restoration was made...it was no longer a hidden agenda.

Care to Correct

There is a place for guidance, open candid communication. I believe the Scriptures called it, "rebuke". We find in Proverbs the difference between a faithful wounding (words of instruction) from a friend and the "kiss of death" from someone who intends to deepen the pain.

> **Proverbs 27:5-6,** *"Open rebuke is better than secret love. Faithful are the wounds of a friend; but the kisses of an enemy are deceitful."*

We cannot confuse "Open Rebuke" with public exposure. Pretenders usually grandstand while a friend will bring instruction in a more discrete setting. One must give place for correction but not to embarrass or add to the already heavy burden being carried.

The key is that it is better to rebuke, give instruction, out in the open…or with no hidden agendas…than to love someone and never express it. The words "Open" and "secret" are key to bringing healing in any situation. Be open…make that call…stop by to see them…go out of your way if you love them. Even at the risk of a candid conversation…reach to those who are hurting. The results will be restoration.

Valiant Men Give Dignity To Brethren

> *1 Samuel 31:12,* "*All the valiant men arose, and went all night, and took the body of Saul and the bodies of his sons from the wall of Bethshan, and came to Jabesh, and burnt them there.*"

You will notice that this is an act of valiant men. The weak will throw under the bus, but those that are strong will bear up the weak. Even though Saul was no longer anointed of God, his fellows could ill afford to allow his demise to be on public display. Because their own reputation was at stake, the valiant men gave dignity to their brother. May we be valiant men and women of God!

As I consider the end of 1 Samuel, my heart is heavy (literally). I read of Jonathan falling to the enemy. The close friend to David has fallen. It was no wonder that Jonathan and David's hearts were knit together, for Jonathan was of like spirit and mind. If it were not for his father's failures he could have been a man after God's own heart as well. Not many would run up a hill toward a garrison of enemy soldiers with nothing but an armor bearer and God! But, because of another's miscues he too lost his life, by association.

Even though Saul deserved the punishment of death, it still saddens me to see a man that had started out with such great potential to fail so miserably. You never see David gloating in Saul's failures, so why should we?

Saul had two issues; 1) Insecurity, 2) Lack of respect for the details when it came to spiritual things. He hid among the stuff when he should have been honored to step onto the stage trusting in God's will and purpose. But, the bottom line was that his insecurity was rooted in an insecure relationship with the Almighty.

After many failures, Saul finds himself stricken with an arrow. Fearful and alone, save his faithful armor bearer, he falls on his

own sword. How fitting of an end to his life's story.
Symbolically, Saul's self destruction eventually took all. The
enemy finds him and cuts off his head, sending it around the
country side to mock. It isn't enough for the enemy to use Saul's
demise to brag to the people, but they also defy God by putting
his failures on display before their idols. What humiliation!

Even though Saul was no longer anointed of God, his fellows
could ill afford to allow his demise to be on public display.
Because their own reputation was at stake, the valiant men gave
dignity to their brother. When a brother or sister fails, it is a
reflection of the whole. We have seen it time and time again. It
is found that a TV evangelist has moral issues and immediately
the organizations that they are affiliated with are brought into
question, and all denominations of Christianity will take yet
another black eye.

To be considered valiant it requires an act that goes over and
above to spare the dignity of someone that doesn't necessarily
deserve it. Go the extra mile, removing them from public
display, providing space to burn the past. Giving the one
needing restored a place of rest, which they may not deserve.

May we be valiant men and women today!

Corvettes In The Pit

When the showroom floor collapsed at the Corvette headquarters
in Bowling Green KY, swallowing up seven very expensive
corvettes, many took notice. Thousands came to view the
sinkhole caused by the collapse of an underground cave.
Hundreds of people were involved in decision making on how to
best remove these expensive vehicles. Causing the least damage
possible was the goal! The first car to be hoisted out was a 2009
ZR1 Blue Devil that only had minor damage to the exterior and
an oil line that had ruptured. A large crowd gathered to watch as
they pulled this first car out and after it was examined and fired
up for the first time the crowd broke out in an applause, with
cheers they expressed their thankfulness for a car that was just
brought 50 feet out of a hole in the ground.
My response is…oh that we could work this diligently to restore
people that have fallen and that those looking on could cheer as
they did when an engine started and ran!

The Spirit of Restoration needs to consume us! Seeking and saving that which was lost. One has to be in the fold for them to be lost. Restoration is needed in many more areas than just personal failure or sin, it is needed when folks loose their health, during loss of a loved one, or even a time of crisis with their children going astray. The feelings of "what could I have done differently" or "where did I go wrong" all lead to "I am not capable…"

"My view was very different from this side. From the outside looking in, from the bottom looking up was a whole new angle for me. Looking for the light, but swallowed in my darkness, I found loneliness my constant but unwanted companion.

My own choices and new circumstances left me an outsider with my family and my faith. Dazed and confused by the looks of some, the caustic comments of a few, the deafening silence of my IPhone made me question if I had a real friend left in the whole world. But when a handful of people did reach out to me, it awakened an unabated desire in me to be a part of community, a community of family, faith, and friends. I truly desire to be whole, to be healed, but I needed to know, first of all, if somebody cared. Enough. Enough to act."

--Kevin, 25 years of ministry and leadership

Restore them…don't patch with duct tape and baling wire…restore back to the original state so that the Kingdom will prosper! Don't spare expense, time, energy, effort!! Do all you can to restore dignity to your brother….first!

CHAPTER 13

When All Is Lost

I can truly concur with David in that there comes a time when your only source of peace is to encourage yourself in the Lord.

> *1 Samuel 30:6*, *"And David was greatly distressed; for the people spake of stoning him, because the soul of all the people was grieved, every man for his sons and for his daughters: but David encouraged himself in the LORD his God"*

David and his men had returned to Ziklag to find that all that they had; wives, children, and homes, had been stolen from them. David was "greatly distressed", as were all those that followed him. What a setback! How could this happen to someone that was anointed of God?!

Here is David, anointed to be king over Israel, standing at the threshold of fulfilling his purpose in life and he, and those closest to him, are grieved at what seemed to be a complete loss!

While they stared at the smoke floating upward, to be caught in the hot desert breeze and wisped away, the Lord is working on removing the thing that prohibits David from stepping into his calling as king over all Israel. In the same hour, Saul is running from the Philistine's, pierced with a fatal wound from an enemy's arrow; he is calling out for someone who would finish him off with a sword.

David is about to be stoned by his brethren…and he encourages himself in the Lord his God.

The contrasts between Saul and David could not be more vivid than at this very moment! One is falling on his own sword while the other stands up, lifts his hands toward heaven and begins to encourage himself "in" the Lord. Stones may start flying at any moment, but, David is determined to lift his eyes to the hills from whence cometh his strength!

If you are at a point where all have turned away from you and those closest to you seem to be stolen away by confusion and turmoil, encourage yourself in the Lord! God is working out the victory as you watch everything going up in smoke. Begin to sing "Victory, victory shall be mine…"!

Two things we find about David…

- He loved God
- He loved the things that God loved.

The combination made him a man that pursued the very heartbeat of God.

David Did Not Gloat Over The Demise of His Enemies

We find two accounts where messengers came to David with news of his enemies being slain. Opportunist who believed they would be rewarded with banquets…made guest of honor…showered with accolades and praise for bravery in hastily bringing good tidings of great joy! Instead, they are met with wails, groans, and a tearing of garments as David falls to morn the loss of life.

Even though it was Saul who chased David all over the country side, David never gloated in the demise of one that had been anointed of God.

May I interject that you will never be known as "after the heart of God" if you are pleased when a Holy Ghost filled child of God has fallen.

> **2 Samuel 4:9-11**, *"And David answered Rechab and Baanah his brother, the sons of Rimmon the Beerothite, and said unto them, As the LORD liveth, who hath redeemed my soul out of all adversity, When one told me, saying, Behold, Saul is dead, thinking to have brought good tidings, I took hold of him, and slew him in Ziklag, who thought that I would have given him a reward for his tidings: How much more, when wicked men have slain a righteous person in his own house upon his bed? shall I not therefore now require his blood of your hand, and take you away from the earth?"*

Two lessons to glean from this passage;

1) David knew that his redemption came from the Lord and not from the hands of men.
2) Don't come to me bragging about how you destroyed my adversaries. I have left them in a Just God's hands, and so should you.

Equal to his pursuit of God, willingness to fall in repentance or to worship Jehovah, these qualities were those that made David a man after God's own heart.

Cold Hearts Fall To Temptation

Not one of us can claim exemption. When the condition of one's heart has moved away from the fires of a Holy God, the enemy will have greater advantage to tempt with fear and pride.

We find in 2 Samuel chapter 24 where David is tempted to number the people. We must note that...

- Numbering the people, in it's self is not a sin. Moses did it twice. We could ask, "Shouldn't the shepherd know the number of sheep, to insure none are lost?"
- Though indirectly, God did not instruct or tempt David to number the people. 1 Chronicles 21:1 provides a parallel account of what led up to David's numbering of the people. It clearly states that "Satan" had tempted David to number the people.

We can only conclude that the state of David's heart was somewhat cold and indifferent with God, leaving an inroad for fears and insecurity to become the perfect environment for temptation.

David had not inquired of the Lord, and he looked at the odds. The obvious conclusion was to assume that Israel was outnumbered.

David did not number the people to insure all were safe and secured within the boarders. He felt the need to only number those that were capable to fight...no draft dodgers would be allowed.

> **2 Samuel 24:9**, *"And Joab gave up the sum of the number of the people unto the king: and there were in Israel eight hundred thousand valiant men that drew the sword; and the men of Judah were five hundred thousand men."*

The act reflected a heart that needed repentance, for it could not see through the lens of faith…only flesh.

> **Hebrews 11:6**, *"But without faith it is impossible to please him: for he that cometh to God must believe that he is, and that he is a rewarder of them that diligently seek him."*

Once again we see where David earns the title of "man after God's own heart". As soon as he realizes that his actions were not pleasing to God he began to repent!

> **2 Samuel 24:10**, *"And David's heart smote him after that he had numbered the people. And David said unto the LORD, I have sinned greatly in that I have done: and now, I beseech thee, O LORD, take away the iniquity of thy servant; for I have done very foolishly."*

It wasn't just that David had gotten caught! No crocodile tears or finger pointing at others to get the heat off his back. He took full responsibility for his actions and admitted his foolishness.

We find the prophet Dan giving David three choices;

1) Seven years of famine
2) Three months at the mercy of his enemies
3) Three days of pestilence in the land

David may have been born at night but it wasn't last night!

As he looked at the three choices he began to realize the weight of his failure. The small window of indifference now comes to rest on his shoulders. Looking back, I'm sure he wished he had not been cold in spirit and had inquired of the Lord before acting…but, now, the reality was that the people now would bear the burden of his ignorance.

David contemplates the loss of life for his people and decides to fall on the mercies of the God that he knew loved them by choosing the one plague that he felt would save the most lives. He could not bare to see the people starving for seven years…slow painful death by the thousands. Nor could he bare the thought of his enemies taking their vengeance out on the innocent men, women, and children…so he picks the one plague that he knew he could fall in repentance and plead for God's mercy upon the people.

Cultivation Cannot Stop

It may seem that we have began to deviate from the core subject of this book. I would respond that the caring spirit has to continue to be cultivated in our lives.

Solomon, when crowned king, had the heart of God. Flirting with idols caused him to fall. There is no doubt that he loved God but "circumstances" required that he build a grove here and there to appease those around him…it won't hurt to go along with them for moral support only…right?

> *1 Kings 11:4*, *"For it came to pass, when Solomon was old, that his wives turned away his heart after other gods: and his heart was not perfect with the LORD his God, as was the heart of David his father."*

A little leaven leaveneth the whole lump…it doesn't take much to permeate through the whole loaf. A little seasoning goes a long way!

Sadly, Solomon's story ends with the people under such heavy taxation that the next generation has to deal with it. Somewhere along the line the building of monuments and houses became more important than the welfare of the people.

If Solomon would have kept a heart for the things of God he would not have been so inclined to lay such heavy burdens upon the people. At the end of his life the comparison is made between he and David…and it was summed up, "…*his heart was not perfect with the Lord his God, as was the heart of David his*

117

father."

The King In Me!

King Saul threw spears at David because he could. He was king, so who in their right mind would think that the king was in the wrong? Surely David deserved the darts that were cast his way…it's the king!

David had no recourse when it came to the spears being thrown his way. First, the king desired him to come and play his harp to sooth his evil heart. Everyone knows that you cannot summons a king. Right? Secondly, it wouldn't be proper for David to pull the spear out of the wall and return the favor by throwing it back at the king. It just isn't a respectable thing to do…and absolutely forbidden! Honor the position…or, be assumed rebellious.

So, David accepted the fact that he was in a training session of dodging spears. You never know when you'll need that skill out on the battle field some day…

I just wonder if David's formative years with Saul were not so impressionable that he made conscience or subconscious decisions to never use his position as a "get out of jail free" ticket. When Abner sought peace, David was so inclined to go soft on him. When his own son, Absolom, rebelled, again, he extended mercy at chagrin of those around him. Many examples of David's reluctance to assert his kingly authority seemed to make him vulnerable to those that would use him. Yet he continued to give others room for humanity to have differing opinions.

Our sinful traits lead us into selfishness, and our defense mechanism is to pretend we are above it all. It becomes the "king in me" that tends to throw spears at others. We begin to take every advantage to get our way.

We must ask, "Do I throw darts at others…because I can?" If so, its time to be the servant that God has desired us to be and seek to love a soul as God loves them.

"You can stand tall without standing on someone. You can be a victor without having victims" ~ Harriet Woods

Heart Change

As Joseph stood before his brothers, who had sold him into slavery, he comforted them with these words...

> ***Genesis 50:20***, *"But as for you, ye thought evil against me; but God meant it unto good, to bring to pass, as it is this day, to save much people alive."*

It is not in us to completely understand how that God uses the will of man to accomplish his purpose for our lives.

> ***Romans 8:28***, *"And we know that all things work together for good to them that love God, to them who are the called according to his purpose."*

When it says "all things" I have to believe that it "means what it says and says what it means"..."ALL THINGS" God will use the good and bad to work his good will and purpose in us. If you are "the called" and willing to submit to the "according to his purpose", then God will orchestrate all situations in our lives to work to our good. It may not feel good, but the sovereign, all knowing, Father of the universe will use them all to make us into what he needs and desires us to be.

The Psalmist said it like this...

> ***Psalms 119:67-71***, *"Before I was afflicted I went astray: but now have I kept thy word. Thou art good, and doest good; teach me thy statutes. The proud have forged a lie against me: but I will keep thy precepts with my whole heart. Their heart is as fat as grease; but I delight in thy law. It is good for me that I have been afflicted; that I might learn thy statutes."*

If it were not for these afflictions that come our way how much would we pray? They tend to drive us to think on the Lord. I/We need these reminders at times to help us re-focus upon what God would have for our lives. To study his precepts with our whole heart!

Don't let it be said of you that *"Their heart is as fat as grease"*! Prospered, stuck on health, striving for property, influence, comforts of all kind! Fat as grease! Spiritually anemic and insensible!

That is exactly what we become if we have not fixed our heart on the laws of God!

> **Hebrews 12:11**, *"Now no chastening for the present seemeth to be joyous, but grievous: nevertheless afterward it yieldeth the peaceable fruit of righteousness unto them which are exercised thereby."*

Isn't that the truth! Who enjoys a good whoop'n? I don't ever recall saying "Awwww, what joy!" as my dad was laying that belt of his on my back side! But chastening will yield peaceable fruit in us.

The "cultivating" theme reminds us of this chastening. The breaking up of the fallow ground, for the purpose of producing more. I've felt like a disk just ran over me before! But my spirit is broken and I am humbled before God so that he can build me up.

No one said it was enjoyable! But, it is profitable.

When you get to the point where you are asking "who cares", you begin to narrow down to a very close circle of people that don't just care, but know how to show they care.

It may get to the point where we do not see where anyone cares whether we live or die. In those times it must drive us to our knees in prayer, and to a deeper sense of worship of God, as well as a more intense study of Scripture to find rest for our soul.

This testing is intended to determine if you have the "salt" to live for God no matter who is with you or not.

When we observe others going through their trial it should stir us to realize that our lack of action is an action in it's self.

As they say, no vote is a vote for evil. When we shake our head and do not understand what a friend is going through, it is not a good time to distance or walk away.

Friendships are built through adversity.

Naturally!

> *Phillipians 2:20-21, "For I have no man likeminded, who will naturally care for your state. For all seek their own, not the things which are Jesus Christ's."*

Even Paul had a challenge in finding men that were like minded, as he and of Jesus Christ. The majority "seek their own" and fail to willingly, without second guessing, "naturally care for your state".

We fight the same battles today in the world and in the church. Finding people who have a heart to care for others more than a pulpit, spot light, money, fame, or fortune has become challenging. Most, sadly, will seek their own desires first, and IF people will get them to their goal then they will use them.

"Lord, help us to love humanity as much as you do."

Remember, he went as far as to die for you...Jesus loved you that much!

How's My Conduct

You've saw the sticker on the back of semis, trucks, and buses..."How's my driving? Call 1-800......" It is the feedback from those who observe how the driver is doing his/her job that will affect our evaluation. Now, when's the last time you called that number and told the company, "Hey, your driver is awesome! He uses his turn signal, and is courteous to others..." No! Its only when they are irresponsible and just about ran you off the road. So, there is always a certain amount of grace that a company gives their drivers. Assuming that no news is good news and if the complaints do not happen too frequently then all is well.

Some evaluations are reminders of how we are doing with our jobs. It never hurts to reflect back and take an honest look at what we've done...looking at the number of complaints as well as the type of feedback that has been given.

The Apostle Paul felt inclined to remind the saints in Thessalonica of his conduct while with them. (*1 Thessalonians 2:1-12*) *An honest self evaluation will help us insure we are maintaining a heart that is in tune with the heartbeat of God.*

Paul pleads his own cause. It shows me that we all feel the need to defend our character at times. For the right reasons, it can be beneficial to remind ourselves and others of our conduct. Keep in mind though, the feedback may tell us otherwise. And, you will only get the feedback from those that have been offended by your conduct enough to "call in".

Paul was "shamefully entreated" when he first came into the region of Thessalonica, yet his conduct was not to spew out the treatment that he had received from others. What really catches my attention is the way he describes himself and his actions. This rough, domineering, sometimes head strong and opinionated, devoted learner of the law has some qualities that could only come from the Holy Spirit.

Paul's personality traits were over ridden by the needs at hand...his affection for the souls of men is shown through these verses. Like an affectionate daddy with his son or daughter...the first time he picks that baby up, it is with nervousness...taking every precaution not to harm the child. The head is wobbling, with no strength in the neck and at times you don't know if it's the diaper or the tummy that is needing attention, but, you hover over the soul and care for it until it can fend for its self.

Perhaps some of the same traits came natural to David, or I'm more inclined to believe that experiences provided the pathway to David becoming a man after God's own heart. It took bears, lions, spears, rejection, hunger, battles, conflicts, friends and children turning their back on him to find his way to know the heartbeat of God.

Get The Goods

> *Matthew 25:14*, *"For the kingdom of heaven is as a man travelling into a far country, who called his own servants, and delivered unto them his goods."*

Jesus is giving his disciples various word pictures that will help them understand what the "kingdom of heaven" is like. The above glimpse of heaven has changed my prayers.

The man that went away to a far country is representative of Jesus leaving his earthly habitation, leaving the disciples without his physical presence to guide them each day.

This passage goes on to discuss talents and three servants success and failure to increase the master's economy.

I've often wondered why a loving God would give "talents" so unequally, and then judge one so harshly that felt inferior to others who were much more talented. I've took it a little personal at times, as I'm sure most who read this book would as well. The "one talent guy" had the odds stacked against him…or so we have preached it.

What is a talent? It is simply the weight that balances out the cost of goods. For instance, if I want a pound of flower it will cost a certain weight (talent) of silver or gold to purchase it. So, I conclude the focus isn't talents as we know them.

The man gave of his own goods to his own servant, based on their "several abilities". This could also be interpreted as "several experiences". With that understanding, I would propose that the master gave a measure of his goods based on the experiences of each servant.

He gave of his goods….God's economy isn't as we tend to seek. His economy is based on love, joy, peace…goodness, mercy…all those things that are found in His Spirit.

When the Lord opened my eyes to this revelation, I was overwhelmed to know that when Jesus went away he sent the Comforter that he could provide "the Goods" from God's economy!

I have, through the empowerment of the Holy Spirit, received the economy of God himself. Not that I am God, but that He dwells within me to do his will and purpose.
The man goes on a journey, leaves me with his goods, based on the experiences that I walk through. Some experiences only require one talent worth of joy…other experiences require two

talents worth of peace, love, and longsuffering…and others hit us like a ton of bricks and require an abundant measure of goodness!

I don't know how so many go through their trials in life without the Comforter to guide them, strengthen, and help them!

The man goes on his journey, gives of his goods to his servants base on the experiences they are incurring, and now what shall they do with these goods? There is a responsibility placed on every individual that has went through a trial and received equaling amounts of joy and peace….we are required to turn to others and increase goodness, mercy, love, joy, and comfort, through the empowerment of the Holy Ghost!

If we do not use the goods that God has placed in our hands to give increase to the Kingdom by lifting up another, we have missed the economy of God and why he gives us of his goods. Its not that we make it through alone, but that we take it to our neighbor and share with them the same joy and peace we have received through our trial.

To pursue the heart of God we must take all these benefits, that have been poured out in our lives, and instead of just going to church and dancing and testifying about how privileged we are, we must go out into the world and share the heart of God with others!

Its God's economy…this kingdom of heaven…not human economy, that we share with a lost and dying world!

CHAPTER 14

The sports headlines on May 2012 was consumed with the news of Junior Seau, NFL Linebacker, dies at age 43 in an apparent suicide. A star athlete with everything going for him...twelve time Pro Bowler, thirteen season veteran in the NFL, one of the most popular players on his team, selected by the Pro Football Hall of Fame as the 1990's "All-Decade Team".

We have had to ask this question every time we hear of such sad news, "How could this happen?" Those closest to him are in complete shock!

These stories surface and yet there are millions of people that stand on the brink of disaster every day. Who cares? Those who claim to have the answers to life's most difficult problems must stand in the gap. But, how do we reach them? Or, perhaps we should ask, why aren't they coming to Christians before they end it all? It leads me to ask, does the world really believe we care?

I'm sure there are those that do, but when mixed all together, Christianity doesn't look or act much different than the world. So, the perception is that if there is no hope in the world there would be no greater hope if they turned to Christianity for the answers to their complex problems.

Cultivating a Culture of Caring must result in giving something that the world could not give. Not better...or an improved version...but truly a caring attitude that is Divine. This, would change the perceptions that are prevalent in this day.

One of the greatest diseases is to be nobody to anybody.
~ Mother Teresa

Give A Drink

> ***Mark 9:41***, *"For whosoever shall give you a cup of water to drink in my name, because ye belong to Christ, verily I say unto you, he shall not lose his reward."*

It never fails when we stop by some friend's home they will say,

"Would you like some tea?" Though a simple act of kindness, there are times that a glass of ice tea really hits the spot. They may not fix it exactly like I would at home, but, it still wets the whistle!

A simple act of offering a cup of water brings dividends beyond our human understanding. A glass of water will not only refresh the recipient, it will start or maintain friendships, and, the rewards are heavenly! Why? Because it is God's desire that we emanate what he does...reach to comfort humanity.

All Have Sinned

Most all professing Christians can quote Romans 3:23, *"All have sinned, and come short of the glory of God."*

There is not one of us that doesn't need some serious cultivating!

If we are breathing, we have failed to care for someone that needed our words and actions of encouragement.

It takes a balance...the anti-social will tell you to leave human contact and cleave to the Holy Spirit, while the socially inclined will require human interaction at every moment of the day. As stated, it requires a balance.

As you have probably gathered thus far in this book, I'm convinced that God requires us to cultivate our interaction with humanity, because it is his "crown jewel" on this earthly project. He desired interaction with willing partners, so shouldn't we?

From the very creation of the first man until today, God has set forth a pattern in which it screams care for your neighbor!

One Man's Junk Is Another Man's Treasure

You've heard that phrase before, I'm sure. Use the clothes, tools, appliances, dishes, fishing tackle, toys, or furniture until we get tired of it and its time to have a rummage sale or give it to the local resale shop. Clean out the shed or garage so we can refill it with the same junk...there's always more "toys" to purchase that are bigger and better. Right?

Unfortunately, we tend to do the same with people. Use them but when they show a little wear, or the shine has faded its time to move along to bigger and better models. Trade that old car even if the payments quadruple! It doesn't smell new any more so it must be time!

Humanity is not a commodity! It's a SOUL!

I'm sure this is preaching to the choir and we all are rolling our eyes or busy shoveling the message over our shoulder to the next guy in line that really needs to hear this…but, I'm here to tell you we all need to hear it!

There is a long line of people we have prejudged as "unworthy" of my time. While singing "Red, yellow, black, or white, they are precious in his sight…" the tendency is to harbor a preconceived idea that this individual isn't worth the energy it would take to pick them up, brush them off, heal their wounds, and lead them to the cross.

Remember God views humanity as the most precious commodity, even when we have used them and now they are used up or too old or not relevant or as simple as I don't agree with them any more, God still views them as gold. Not a pot that can be sold in an auction for a couple of bucks just to make room for another vessel.

When dignity and self worth are crushed, whoa to them that seek to cast away. Differences of opinions can be had, but, readily discarding a soul as no longer worthy of my time, is an atrocity against God.

It Ain't Natural

> *Philippians 2:20-21, "For I have no man likeminded, who will naturally care for your state. For all seek their own, not the things which are Jesus Christ's."*

Even Paul had a challenge in finding men that were like minded. The majority "seek their own" and fail to willingly, without second guessing, "naturally care for your state". We fight the same battles today in the world and in the church. It becomes increasingly rare to find Christians who will care for others more than a pulpit, spot light, money, fame, or fortune. Most, sadly, will seek their own desires first, and IF people will get them to their goal then they will use them. Lord, help us to love humanity as much as you do. Remember, he went as far as to die for you...Jesus loved you that much!

Worse Than Bitter Water

> **James 3:11**, *"Doth a fountain send forth at the same place sweet water and bitter?"*

James draws a word picture to help us understand that we cannot love God and despise man. In God's eyes we either love God and humanity, or we despise them both.

The only thing worse is when an individual shuts off the water all together. It is a tool of the devil himself to pretend that we love and communicate with God and shut off the valve of communication with those around us. The silent treatment is a desert...if bitter water flows out at least there is a cleansing of the one pouring out and a watering (though bitter at the time) to bring life to the growth in a person's life. To shut off all communication, or give the cold shoulder, is in its self a way to kill the very life of a person.

Life and death is in the tongue...use it to give life abundantly.

Don't Be A Fake

> *"I value the friend who for me finds time on his calendar, but I cherish the friend who for me does not consult his calendar."*
> *~ Robert Brault*

Nothing worse than finding out a friend had shallow limits to their love for you. After years of enjoying a relationship with another person, only to find out they had not been genuine in their love. Finding that a friend's intentions were self serving, and lacked in sincerity can be devastating. This realization is a punch to the gut that no one could really explain. You can only double up and absorb the blow until such a time that the initial shock subsides and you are able to again stand up straight again.

Romans 12:9-10 helps us to avoid such a blow...

"Let love be without dissimulation. Abhor that which is evil; cleave to that which is good Be kindly affectioned one to another with brotherly love; in honour preferring one another."

"Without dissimulation" simply put means to be sincere. Don't be a hypocrite about your love to others. If we could live our lives with a pure love for others it would remove all possibility of such disappointments. Be pure, be sincere, and be truthful in your love.

"Kindly affectioned" is defined as; cherishing one's kindred, especially parents or children; fond of natural relatives, that is, fraternal towards fellow Christians.

Blood does run thicker than water!

Good and evil are weighed in the balance of brotherly love. The weights are "dissimulation", "kindly affectioned", "honour", and "preferring another". Tip the scale in the wrong way and evil will rule.

TF Tenney ~ "To be right satisfies the ego. To be kind satisfies God."

Grow Up!

We've all used that term, or at least thought it when you desired a different result or action. But, in this caring business, if truth be told, most of us have grown up too much.

A child can go to a Johnny or Susie's house and have a falling out that would make world war three look small, but by the next Sunday they are begging their parents to let them go back to their friend's house.

I remember some of my best buddies and I, in our childhood days, would be down in the dirt going at it on a regular basis. But, by the end of the day we were still friends and having a blast.

When you tell someone "Grow Up!" you may be asking for more than you bargained for. It seems that grown up people are much slyer with their jabs, and instead of coming out with their thoughts they put them in cute phrases and doll them up so that they still hurt but there is no recourse for the one receiving the punishment. When the recipient reacts in a negative way it appears to everyone else that they need to "Grow Up!" But when they grow up, they learn to use words to cut the other even more deeply.

I'm not sure I would ask you to "Grow Up!" in the sense of caring. For children don't see color of skin, or even ask how much money you make, or find fault with the way you dress, or critique your physical features…if you cry, they cry with you! You've heard it…one baby starts crying in church and before you know it the church is full of crying babies! And, I'm not referring to the grown ups!

Become mature in the natural and in the knowledge of Christ Jesus our Lord, but don't grow out of caring for others when they fall, are hurt, or just have a bad day. Find a way to go back over to their house and play games…it might be to our advantage to never "Grow Up!"

Why Friends?

Friends don't let friends go down the road of life alone…

> ***Ecclesiastes 4:9-10***, *"Two are better than one; because they have a good reward for their labour. For if they fall, the one will lift up his fellow: but woe to him that is alone when he falleth; for he hath not another to help him up."*

There is power in multiplicity. Friendships should add to our strength, not take away. If a friendship is ever all giving or all taking, it isn't healthy.

We truly find out who our friends are when we fall…fellows will lift up. Woe to him that has no one who will come along beside them and lift up when we fall.

Tommy Tenney tweeted what friends do…

F orgive you.
R espect you.
I nspire you.

130

E ncourage you.
N ourish you.
D efend you.
S upport you.

Who Is Righteous?

I will close with this last thought that the Lord gave me as I was finishing up this book.

Matthew 25:31-46 provides a glimpse of what the final judgment day will be like. You've read it many times so I will simply provide some highlights.

First we know that all nations are gathered before the "Son of man" and he will sit on "the throne of his glory". He will separate "one from another"...no mention of asking opinions, I'm of the opinion that he already knows our opinions...sheep on the right and goats on the left, speaking first to the sheep by complimenting them for their concern for the basic human needs of giving meat, drink, taking in strangers, clothing the naked, concerning themselves with the sick, and visiting those who have messed up in society and have found themselves in prison.

The "righteous" responded, when did we do these things and the King answered, "Inasmuch as ye have done it unto one of the least of these my brethren, ye have done it unto me"

Those that were considered goats were judged for the same yet they had fallen short on caring for humanity as the King had desired.

Take note that this passage made no mention of a basic plan of salvation. I have to consider the thought that all who were there on judgment were those who had been "born again", but the dividing line came when the King took note of their performance in caring for humanity as he did.

I ask you how important is it to Cultivate a Culture of Caring? Perhaps it will have eternal implications...

Re-published in January of 2013, this book will inspire through thoughts of miracles and personal experiences in the life of Dwight L Hardin. _Many testimonies have been given of how this book has lifted the broken, strengthened the weak, and provided an assurance to the hurting, that there is a Savior who cares for their every need._ _Be encouraged through the thoughts shared by the author._

Published in May of 2013, this book will break down the beatitudes as a practical application to every believer's life. _This project was a burden by the author, Dwight L Hardin, to help every born again Christian to live a complete life in Christ Jesus our Lord._ _It doesn't pull any punches...but it is certainly done in and with love._

More projects to come by Dwight L Hardin...

These books can be purchased by contacting:

Mark A Hardin (Publisher)
1918 Pheasant Rd
Xenia, IL 62899
_Ph# 618-292-7415_

Or by going online to: www.CreateSpace.com

Made in the USA
San Bernardino, CA
28 July 2014